Bulletin
of the European Union

Supplement 14/97

Commission opinion on the Czech Republic's application for membership of the European Union

Document drawn up on the basis of COM(97) 2009 final

European Commission

A great deal of additional information on the European Union is available on the Internet.
It can be accessed through the Europa server (http://europa.eu.int)

Cataloguing data can be found at the end of this publication

Luxembourg: Office for Official Publications of the European Communities, 1997

ISBN 92-828-1226-X

© European Communities, 1997
Reproduction is authorized provided the source is acknowledged

Printed in Belgium

PRINTED ON CHLORINE-FREE BLEACHED PAPER

CORRIGENDA

Supplement 14/97 to the Bulletin of the EU

Czech Republic

On pages 87 and 98, the tables should be replaced by the following tables (corrected figures are shown in negative).

Page 87:

Present Composition of the Parliament of the Czech Republic

Political Party		Chamber Seats	Chamber %	Senate Seats	Senate %
Civil Democratic Party	ODS	68	33	32	39.5
Civic Democratic Alliance	ODA	13	7	7	8.6
Christian Democratic Party	KDU-CSL	18	9	13	16.0
Social Democratic Party	CSSD	61	31	25	30.8
Republican Party	SPR-RSC	18	11		
Communist Party of Bohemia and Moravia	KSCM	22	9	2	2.5
Democratic Union	DEU			1	1.2
Independents				1	1.2
		200		81	

Main Economic Indicators

	1990	1991	1992	1993	1994	1995	1996
	\multicolumn{7}{c}{In percentage change over the previous year}
Inflation rate	9.7	56.5	11.1	20.8	10	9.1	8.8
	\multicolumn{7}{c}{Previous year = 100}
Industrial production volume indices				94.7	102.1	109.2	106.8
Gross agricultural production volume indices				97.7	94.0	105.0	
Unemployment rate (ILO methodology)	\multicolumn{7}{c}{In % labour force}
Total				3.9	3.8	3.6	3.4
Less than 25 years					7.7	6.8	6.1
25 years and more					3	2.9	2.9
	\multicolumn{7}{c}{In billions of USD}
Gross foreign debt				4.548	5.838		
Balance of payments	\multicolumn{7}{c}{In millions of USD}
Exports of goods				12 997.2	14 016.4	21 462.4	21 702.5
Imports of goods				–13 308.9	–14 905.3	–25 140.3	–27 674.3
Trade balance				–311.8	–888.8	–3 677.8	–5 971.8
Services, net				1 010.7	733.0	1 842.0	1 785.1
Income, net				–117.4	–20.2	–105.7	–679.9
Current account balance				669.2	–49.7	–1 369.1	–4 476.4
Capital and fin. acc. (excl. reserves)				2 470.0	3 371.1	8 232.6	4 072.3
Reserve assets				–3 029.3	–2 371.6	–7 458.1	828.0

Contents

A — Introduction 9

a) Preface 9

Application for Membership 9
Context of the Opinion 9
Contents of the Opinion 9

b) Relations between the European Union and the Czech Republic 10

Historical and Geopolitical Context 10
The Czech Republic's Position concerning the European Union 11
Contractual Relations 11
Pre-Accession Strategy 12
Trade Relations 13
General Evaluation 13

B — Criteria for Membership 15

1. Political Criteria 15

1.1. Democracy and the Rule of Law 15

Parliament and Legislative Powers: Structure 15
Functioning of Parliament 16
The Executive: Structure 16
Functioning of the Executive 16
The Judiciary: Structure 17
Functioning of the Judiciary 17

1.2. Human Rights and the Protection of Minorities 17

Civil and Political Rights 18
Economic, Social and Cultural Rights 19
Minority Rights and the Protection of Minorities 19

	1.3.	General Evaluation	20
2.		**Economic Criteria**	20
	2.1.	Economic Situation	20
		Background	20
		Liberalisation	21
		Stabilisation of the Economy	23
		Structural Change	24
		Financial Sector	26
		Economic and Social Development	27
	2.2.	The Economy in the Perspective of Membership	28
		Introduction	28
		Existence of a Functioning Market Economy	28
		Capacity to cope with Competitive Pressure and Market Forces	29
		Prospects and Priorities	31
	2.3.	General Evaluation	31
3.		**Ability to assume the Obligations of Membership**	32
	3.1.	Internal Market without Frontiers	32
		The Four Freedoms	33
		— General Framework	33
		— Free Movement of Goods	35
		— Free Movement of Capital	37
		— Free Movement of Services	38
		— Free Movement of Persons	40
		— General Evaluation	41
		Competition	42
	3.2.	Innovation	44
		Information Society	44
		Education, Training and Youth	44
		Research and Technological Development	45
		Telecommunications	46
		Audio-visual	48

	3.3.	**Economic and Fiscal Affairs**	48
		Economic and Monetary Union	48
		Taxation	50
		Statistics	52
	3.4.	**Sectoral Policies**	52
		Industry	52
		Agriculture	55
		Fisheries	58
		Energy	59
		Transport	61
		Small and Medium Enterprises	62
	3.5.	**Economic and Social Cohesion**	63
		Employment and Social Affairs	63
		Regional Policy and Cohesion	64
	3.6.	**Quality of Life and Environment**	65
		Environment	65
		Consumer Protection	66
	3.7.	**Justice and Home Affairs**	67
	3.8.	**External Policies**	70
		Trade and International Economic Relations	70
		Development	71
		Customs	71
		Common Foreign and Security Policy	73
	3.9.	**Financial Questions**	73
		Financial Control	73
		Budgetary Implications	74
4.		**Administrative Capacity to apply the *Acquis***	76
	4.1.	**Administrative Structures**	76

4.2.	**Administrative and Judicial Capacity**	76
4.3.	**General Evaluation**	80

C — Summary and Conclusion 81

Annex 85

    Present Composition of the Parliament of the Czech Republic   87
    Single Market: White Paper Measures   88
    Statistical Data   90

S. 14/97

A — Introduction

a) Preface

Application for Membership

The Czech Republic presented its application for membership of the European Union on 17 January 1996, and the Council of Ministers decided on 29 January 1996 to implement the procedure laid down in Article O of the Treaty, which provides for consultation of the Commission.

That is the framework in which the Commission submits the present Opinion, responding to the request of the European Council in Madrid in December 1995 to present the Opinion as soon as possible after the conclusion of the Intergovernmental Conference, which commenced in March 1996 and concluded in June 1997.

Context of the Opinion

The Czech application for membership is being examined at the same time as applications from nine other associated countries. The Czech Republic's accession is to be seen as part of an historic process, in which the countries of Central and Eastern Europe overcome the division of the continent which has lasted for more than 40 years, and join the area of peace, stability and prosperity created by the Union.

The European Council in Copenhagen in June 1993 concluded that:

'The associated countries in Central and Eastern Europe that so desire shall become members of the Union. Accession will take place as soon as a country is able to assume the obligations of membership by satisfying the economic and political conditions. Membership requires:

☐ that the candidate country has achieved stability of institutions guaranteeing democracy, the rule of law, human rights and respect for and protection of minorities;

☐ the existence of a functioning market economy, as well as the capacity to cope with competitive pressure and market forces within the Union;

☐ the ability to take on the obligations of membership, including adherence to the aims of political, economic and monetary union.

The Union's capacity to absorb new members, while maintaining the momentum of European integration, is also an important consideration in the general interest of both the Union and the candidate countries'.

This declaration spelled out the political and economic criteria for examining the accession requests of the associated countries of Central and Eastern Europe.

The European Council in Madrid in December 1995 referred to the need, in the context of the pre-accession strategy, 'to create the conditions for the gradual, harmonious integration of the applicant countries, particularly through:

☐ the development of the market economy,

☐ the adjustment of their administrative structure,

☐ the creation of a stable economic and monetary environment'.

In its Opinion, the Commission analyses the Czech application on its merits, but according to the same criteria as the other applications, on which it is delivering Opinions at the same time. This way of proceeding respects the wish, expressed by the European Council in Madrid, to ensure that the applicant countries are treated on an equal basis.

In addition to the individual Opinions the Commission is presenting separately to the Council, in the framework of its communication 'Agenda 2000', a general assessment of the accession requests, and its recommendations concerning the strategy for successful enlargement of the Union. At the same time, it is presenting an evaluation of the impact of enlargement on the Union's policies.

Contents of the Opinion

The structure of the Opinion takes account of the conclusions of the European Council in Copenhagen. It:

☐ describes the relations up to now between the Czech Republic and the Union, particularly in the framework of the association agreement;

☐ analyses the situation in respect of the political conditions mentioned by the European Council (democracy, rule of law, human rights, protection of minorities);

☐ assesses the Czech Republic's situation and prospects in respect of the economic conditions mentioned by the European Council (market economy, capacity to cope with competitive pressure);

☐ addresses the question of the Czech Republic's capacity to adopt the obligations of membership, that is the *acquis* of the Union as expressed in the Treaty, the secondary legislation, and the policies of the Union;

☐ makes finally a general evaluation of the Czech Republic's situation and prospects in respect of the conditions for membership of the Union, and a recommendation concerning accession negotiations.

In assessing the Czech Republic in respect of the economic criteria and its capacity to assume the *acquis*, the Commission has included a prospective assessment; it has attempted to evaluate the progress which can reasonably be expected on the part of the Czech Republic in the coming years, before accession, taking account of the fact that the *acquis* itself will continue to develop. For this purpose, and without prejudging the actual date of accession, the Opinion is based on a medium-term time horizon of approximately five years.

During the preparation of the Opinion, the Commission has obtained a wealth of information on the Czech Republic's situation from the Czech authorities, and has utilised many other sources of information, including the Member States and numerous international organisations.

b) Relations between the European Union and the Czech Republic

Historical and Geopolitical Context

The Czech Republic is a landlocked country in the middle of Europe, with flatlands in the centre and a mountainous periphery. Its neighbours are Austria, Germany, Poland and Slovakia. It has an area of 79 000 km^2 and a population of 10,3 million.

For nearly four centuries after 1527, when Ferdinand I of Habsburg was crowned as King of Bohemia, the Czech territories were part of the Austro-Hungarian Empire. Czech aspirations for greater autonomy in the Empire grew during the nineteenth century. The Czechoslovak Republic was proclaimed in October 1918. Its composition was multiethnic: 51% Czech, 23% German, 14% Slovak and 5,5% Hungarian, according to a 1921 census. The country inherited 60-70% of the industrial base of the Austro-Hungarian Empire.

In the 1930s the Sudeten Germans' demands for autonomy created increasing tension. Under the 1938 Munich Agreement and the Vienna Arbitration the regions bordering Germany and mostly settled by Germans were ceded to Germany, and a quarter of the Slovak lands to Hungary. In March 1939 German troops occupied the rest of the Czech lands. After the War the Czechoslovak Republic was restored to its prewar borders, except for Ruthenia, which was annexed by the Soviet Union. The government passed a decree at the end of the war dispossessing Sudeten Germans of their property, and almost all of them were forced to leave Czechoslovak territory.

Czechoslovakia was one of the founding members of the post-war international economic institutions (IMF and IBRD in 1945, GATT in 1948). But after the formation in 1948 of a government composed of only Communists and their allies the Communist party expanded its hold on power. Under the division of labour agreed within Comecon Czechoslovakia concentrated on developing its heavy industry. In the 1960s central controls were partially relaxed. Reform pressures within the Communist Party resulted in the election of Alexander Dubcek as First Secretary in January 1968. The introduction of democratic elements into political and cultural life, known as the Prague Spring, was brought to a brutal end by invasion by members of the Warsaw Pact on 21 August 1968, which led to reimposition of Soviet orthodoxy under Gustav Husak. That year the country also introduced a federal structure, with Czech and Slovak Republics as separate entities.

A small dissident movement, later associated with the Charter 77 group, remained active through the 1970s and 1980s. The political unrest in many countries of Central and Eastern Europe in 1989 led to protests in Czechoslovakia too. Popular reaction to the violent police repression of a student demonstration in Prague on 17 November, and demonstrations in Bratislava, led to Husak's resignation and the election the following month of Vaclav Havel, a leading member of Charter 77, as President. Elections in 1992 led to the formation of a coalition government of centre-right parties committed to rapid economic reform. In 1996 the coalition narrowly failed to win another majority. Though it has been able to form another government, it has had to slow the rate of economic reform.

After 1989, the name of the country was officially changed to the Czech and Slovak Federal Republic. Differences between Czech and Slovak politicians on the future federal structure and economic policy became unbridgeably wide. In October 1992 the parliaments of the two Republics passed a joint resolution dissolving the federation and creating two independent successor states as of 1 January 1993.

The Czech Republic's Position concerning the European Union

'Return to Europe' was one of the central slogans of the political demonstrations of November 1989. The first post-Communist government stated Czechoslovakia's interest in becoming a member of the European Communities in its provisional programme of March 1990. The first Czech government, inaugurated in July 1992, stated that membership of the European Union was the primary goal for an autonomous Czech Republic. The Czech Republic submitted its application for membership on 23 January 1996. The second government of Prime Minister Klaus, installed in July 1996, expressed its commitment to membership as follows: 'the basic orientation and goals of Czech foreign policy remain unchanged, therefore the government will smoothly follow up the foreign policy results of its predecessor. As its main priorities the government sees the quickest possible acquisition of full membership of the EU and NATO by the Czech Republic, considering the fulfilment of these goals to be the completion of our country's transformation from the point of view of foreign policy'.

Contractual Relations

Diplomatic relations between the European Community and the Czechoslovak Republic were established in September 1988. The first agreement between them was the four-year Trade Agreement on industrial products which entered into force in April 1989. A Trade and Cooperation Agreement was concluded in 1990. An Association Agreement, to be known as a Europe Agreement, was signed between the European Communities and Czechoslovakia on 16 December 1991. Its trade provisions entered into force in March 1992 by way of an Interim Agreement replacing the 1989 Agreement. The Interim Agreement provided for the consolidation of previous trade concessions as well as the gradual and asymmetric establishment of a free trade area over a period of ten years.

The dissolution of Czechoslovakia into Czech and Slovak Republics made it necessary to negotiate separate Europe Agreements with the two successor states. The agreement with the Czech Republic was signed in October 1993, and entered into force on 1 February 1995.

The Europe Agreement is now the legal basis for relations between the Czech Republic and the European Union. Its aim is to provide a legal framework for political dialogue, promote the expansion of trade and economic relations between the parties, provide a basis for Community technical and financial assistance, and an appropriate framework to support the Czech Republic's gradual integration into the Union. The institutional framework provides a mechanism for implementation, management and monitoring of all areas of relations. Sub-committees examine questions at a technical level. The Association Committee, at senior official level, provides for in-depth discussion and often finds solutions to problems arising under the Agreement. The Association Council examines the overall status of relations and provides the opportunity to review the Czech Republic's progress in preparing for accession.

A government decree of November 1994 created the Government Committee for European Integration, the supreme decision-making body in matters of European integration. It is headed by the Prime Minister. Permanent members include the Ministers for Finance, Industry and Trade, Agriculture and Foreign Affairs. The Government Committee is supported by a Working Committee of officials chaired by a

Deputy Minister for Foreign Affairs, and underpinned by 23 specialised Working Groups, including one on approximation of legislation.

Pre-Accession Strategy

Implementation of the Europe Agreement and the White Paper

The institutional framework of the Europe Agreement is fully operational. The Association Council and Association Committee have each met three times, and the Joint Parliamentary Association Committee twice yearly. The system of multidisciplinary subcommittees agreed at the end of 1996 is proving its usefulness. Cooperation with the Commission has been close and effective over state aids, industrial and commercial property rights, macro-economic policy, reduction of customs duties and other issues. Differences which have emerged on trade issues have usually been settled satisfactorily within the procedures laid down by the Agreement.

There have, however, been reports since early 1997 of a limited number of products, originating in the Community and conforming to EC standards, not being admitted on to the Czech market. Moreover, the Czech Government introduced in April 1997 an import deposit scheme which is not in conformity with the Europe Agreement. Contacts continue within the procedures laid down by the Agreement to try to resolve these issues.

The Commission's White Paper of 1995 on the Internal Market set out the legislation which candidate countries would have to transpose and implement in order to apply the *acquis* communautaire and identified elements essential to the implementation of the single market (known as Stage I measures) which would need priority attention. The Czech Republic began a systematic process of approximation of its legislation as early as 1991. In early 1995 the Government approved a timetable for approximation. But there is still a long way to go. In response to the White Paper, the Government published in the spring of 1996 its own 'Priorities for the Implementation of the White Paper in the Czech Republic'. This defines key White Paper measures which should have priority up to the year 2000. The document also recognises the need to change and improve administrative structures. New structures are proposed for administration of the environment, direct and indirect taxation, personal data protection and social policy. So far these intentions are yet to be implemented.

The Europe Agreement is for the most part being implemented according to the procedures and timetable laid out in it. There have been few trade problems, though recently important trade-related problems have arisen (notably the import deposit scheme). There is room for enhanced dialogue and cooperation to prevent such issues from developing.

Structured Dialogue

The Czech Republic participates at all levels of the structured dialogue, but considers that meetings should be made more productive by better preparation and a more focused agenda giving more opportunity for extended dialogue with the Commission. The decision of the General Affairs Council of February 1996 to improve preparations is a step in this direction. A priority area for the Czech Republic is Justice and Home Affairs, where it sees insufficient progress. The country would prefer to see a more substantive political dialogue with the Union on a bilateral level within the Association Council.

PHARE

Between 1990 and 1996 433 million ECU was allocated to the Czech Republic. The allocation for 1996 was 54 million ECU. Prime sectors have included private sector development, infrastructure, environment and human resource development. A Cross-Border Cooperation programme in the Czech-German and Czech-Austrian border areas has been operating since 1994. After initial hesitations the Czech authorities have come to see PHARE as an important tool for transforming their economy and preparing their country for accession. But there have been problems related to delays in programme implementation and complications in targeting funds to focus on priority areas.

Participation in Community Programmes

As foreseen under the Europe Agreement, decisions have been taken to permit the Czech Republic to participate in Leonardo, Socrates, Youth for Europe and other programmes in the sectors of training, culture, audio-visual, social and health policy, research and development, energy saving and SMEs.

Trade Relations

Between 1989 and 1992 EC imports from Czechoslovakia jumped from 2,6 billion ECU to 5,5 billion ECU (a jump of 112%); and EC exports from 2,4 billion ECU to 6,3 billion ECU (a jump of 163%). Between 1992 and 1996 the Czech Republic expanded its trade with the Union even further. EU imports increased from 4,9 billion ECU to 9,4 billion ECU (92% up) and EU exports from 6,1 billion ECU to 13,3 billion ECU (up 118%). In 1996 the Union accounted for just over 60% of Czech foreign trade. The Czech Republic accounted for 2,25% of all EU exports and 1,66% of EU imports.

This reorientation of trade and the ability of Czech exports to penetrate new markets suggest that the quality of goods has been rising. But part of their competitive advantage has come from wage levels, initially low but since much raised. Czech exports are highly concentrated, with machinery and transport equipment accounting for 33% of the total, and manufactured goods 29%. The same two categories constitute the largest share of imports, adding up together to 57%. In 1996 exports of manufactured goods, earlier one of the growth areas, contracted.

The Czech Republic has a Customs Union with Slovakia and is one of the initiators of the Central European Free Trade Agreement. Trade with CEFTA partners has consolidated over recent years.

General Evaluation

Since its foundation the Czech Republic has pursued stronger links with the European Union in all fields. The Europe Agreement has been effectively implemented in most sectors. There have been few trade problems, though the still not resolved issue of its import deposit scheme is one exception. Confident of its progress towards meeting the obligations of EU membership, the Czech Republic has at times shown signs of reluctance to acknowledge difficulties and seek a collaborative approach to resolving them.

B — Criteria for Membership

1. Political Criteria

The European Council in Copenhagen decided on a number of 'political' criteria for accession to be met by the candidate countries in Central and Eastern Europe. These countries must achieve 'stability of institutions guaranteeing democracy, the rule of law, human rights and respect for and protection of minorities'.

In carrying out the assessment required in this connection, the European Commission has drawn on a number of sources of information: answers given by the Czech authorities to the questionnaire sent to them by the Commission in April 1996, bilateral follow-up meetings, reports from Member States' embassies and the Commission's delegation, assessments by international organisations (including the Council of Europe and the OSCE), reports produced by non-governmental organisations, etc.

The following assessment involves a systematic examination of the main ways in which the public authorities in each of the candidate countries are organised and operate, and the steps they have taken to protect fundamental rights. It does not confine itself to a formal description but seeks to assess the extent to which democracy and the rule of law actually operate.

This assessment relates to the situation in June 1997. It does not examine in detail any changes which have taken place since the fall of the Communist regime or which may come about in the future, though it generally takes account of any stated intention to reform a particular sector. The situation of the public administration is mentioned here only in passing: it will be examined in greater depth in Chapter 4.

1.1. Democracy and the Rule of Law

The Constitution adopted in December 1992 by the National Council of the Czech Republic, and the Charter of Fundamental Rights which forms an integral part of it, established a parliamentary democracy. The Czech institutions function smoothly, the various authorities showing awareness of their respective areas of competence and of the need for mutual cooperation.

Parliament and Legislative Powers: Structure

The Parliament is a bicameral body — consisting of the Chamber of Deputies and, since November 1996, the Senate — which respectively comprise 200 and 81 members elected by direct universal suffrage. Deputies are elected for 4 years on a proportional representation basis (representation requiring a minimum threshold of 5% of votes cast) and Senators for 6 years by a majority vote spread over two rounds, one-third being renewed every two years. There are no specific rules which guarantee the representation of minorities in the Parliament. The Chamber of Deputies enjoys greater powers than the Senate and may overrule it during the procedure for passing laws (Article 47 of the Constitution). The Government is answerable only to the Chamber of Deputies.

The President of the Republic may dissolve the Chamber of Deputies if the Government fails to win a vote of confidence or if the Chamber of Deputies is no longer able to function normally (Article 35 of the Constitution). Dissolution is not possible in the three months prior to elections to the Chamber.

Members of Parliament are accorded traditional immunities under Article 27 of the Constitution.

The Opposition plays a recognised and participatory role in the functioning of the institutions in the Czech Republic, as demonstrated by the formation of parliamentary committees of enquiry within the Chamber of Deputies (Article 30 of the Constitution) in which each political group is represented in proportion to its total weight in the Chamber. These committees may be chaired by a member of the Opposition.

The Czech Republic is governed on a multi-party basis (54 political parties registered, of which 20 took part in the last elections to the

Chamber of Deputies). The political parties represented in Parliament are funded from the State budget in proportion to the number of members elected.

Parliament is the legislative body and shares the right of initiative with the Government. The latter also has regulatory power, where conferred by the legislator, exclusively for the purpose of implementing laws.

There is no procedure for referenda in the Czech Republic.

Functioning of Parliament

Elections are free and genuine. The elections of June 1996 to the Chamber of Deputies gave victory to the ruling Centre Right coalition (see Annex).

Parliament operates in a satisfactory manner: its powers are respected and the Opposition plays its normal role.

The Executive: Structure

The President of the Republic is elected by Parliament for a 5-year term, renewable once only. He can call upon Parliament to conduct a further reading of a law on which a vote has just been taken, but the Chambers may disregard this veto by a simple majority vote. He enjoys the traditional powers of a Head of State.

The President of the Republic appoints the Prime Minister and, on the latter's proposal, the ministers. The Government, and the ministers individually, are answerable to the Chamber of Deputies. Ministers may also be held liable for crimes and offences committed in pursuance of their functions, except in the case of statements made before the Chambers.

The country is divided administratively into 75 districts administered by representatives appointed by the Government and answerable to the Minister of the Interior. Each ministry, at district level, is subdivided into decentralised departments answerable to the central authority. The district leader is assisted by an assembly comprising representatives of the communes; he may suspend decisions taken by the assembly and call for central government arbitration.

The Czech Constitution provides for two levels of local authority: regions and communes. The former have not yet been set up, but the Government has undertaken to ensure their creation before the year 2000. The number of such regions is currently the subject of debate (between 8 and 13). The communes, of which there are 6233, are run by municipal councils elected by universal franchise for a 4-year term; the councils themselves elect their mayors.

The public service is hindered somewhat by the absence of civil service regulations and the fact that salaries are relatively low, which explains why the most competent staff are leaving it for the private sector. All of these factors add to the difficulty in combating corruption.

Under the 'lustration' purification law which was adopted in 1991 and extended in 1996 up to the year 2000 (after having been sent back to Parliament by the President for further scrutiny), members of, or collaborators with, the former security services and persons who played an active role in the former communist regime are excluded from a number of public service jobs (government and administration, army, security services and police, justice, radio and television and public enterprises).

Under this system the administration issues 'certificates' to any person who so requests, based on records kept by the former security services. Since 1996, any interested person may request access to such documents; this right is no longer confined to the courts for the purposes of legal proceedings.

The army, the secret services and the police fall under civilian control and are subject to the jurisdiction of the civil courts. The secret services are required to report their activities to Parliament.

Functioning of the Executive

The central institutions of the State operate smoothly.

Local authorities continue to encounter difficulties in asserting their autonomy, particularly in respect of funding, as they depend on the State for approximately two-thirds of their budgetary resources.

Application of the 'lustration law' has produced the following results: of the 300 000 certificates requested, only 9 000 (3%) resulted in an exclusion decision; in 580 of these cases the decision was contested and half of the complainants had their exclusions annulled by the courts. The Government has signalled its intention not to extend the system beyond the year 2000.

The police, which is currently undergoing reorganisation, is frequently criticised for the slowness of its investigations and for inefficiency in combating drug-trafficking and the rise in organised crime.

The secret services operate in a manner which would appear to respect the essential rules of democracy. A parliamentary committee of enquiry set up in 1996 to examine possible cases of illegal surveillance of leading figures, political parties and foreign embassies reached the conclusion, at the beginning of 1997, that no such illegalities were being perpetrated.

The Judiciary: Structure

The Czech judiciary is independent. Magistrates are appointed for life by the President of the Republic, on a proposal by the Minister of Justice and on request of the presidents by the courts. They may not be removed from office, nor may they be transferred without their agreement. Equally, they may not be dismissed or suspended except on grounds strictly laid down by law.

The State Prosecutor is appointed by the Government on a proposal by the Minister of Justice, who appoints the other members of the State Prosecutor's Office. They are subject to the hierarchical authority of the Minister.

The scrutiny of administrative measures falls within the competence of the civil courts. Under Article 91 of the Constitution, they come under the authority of an administrative Supreme Court which has yet to be established.

The Czech Republic has no Ombudsman.

The Constitutional Court comprises 15 judges appointed for 10 years by the President of the Republic with the approval of the Senate. The Court scrutinises the conformity of laws and regulations with the Constitution and international treaties. It may also annul measures taken by government authorities if they infringe the autonomy of local authorities.

The Constitutional Court undertakes advance verification of laws (referred by the President of the Republic, 41 Deputies or 17 Senators) and regulations (referred by the Government, 25 Deputies or 10 Senators). It may also scrutinise existing laws either at the request of a court, in the case of a current legal proceedings, or of a private individual who, having exhausted preliminary avenues of appeal, considers his/her fundamental rights to have been infringed. The Court may also refer cases to itself.

Functioning of the Judiciary

The situation of the courts in the Czech Republic constitutes a major challenge for the country's integration into the European Union. The courts are overloaded, numerous cases do not receive a judgement and the average length of commercial law proceedings, for example, exceeds 3 years.

These problems result less from understaffing or inadequate facilities than from inadequate experience and qualification on the part of the judges, who have to apply legislation which frequently is totally new and for which, most often, there is no established legal precedent.

The Constitutional Court plays an important and active role in the operation of the Czech institutions. Since its establishment it has had nearly 4 900 cases referred to it and there has been a large increase in the number of cases since 1995. It has granted approximately 200 petitions. Its decisions on questions of nationality and ownership testify to its role in enforcing the rule of law.

1.2. Human Rights and the Protection of Minorities

The Czech Republic has introduced various internal rules designed to ensure respect for human rights and the rights of minorities. Such protection is also afforded by various international conventions, in the forefront of which is the European Convention for the Protection of Human Rights and its principal additional protocols. Under Article F of the EU Treaty, these texts form part of the *acquis* communautaire and any State wishing to join the European Union must first have ratified them.

The Czech Republic, a member of the Council of the Europe since 1993, has been party to the European Convention for the Protection of

Human Rights and its additional protocols since March 1992, when they were ratified by Czechoslovakia. It also permits individuals to take their case to the European Court if they consider that their rights under this convention have been violated.

The Czech Republic has also ratified various other international conventions on the protection of human rights and the rights of minorities including the Convention on the Prevention of Torture, and has signed but not yet ratified the Framework Convention on National Minorities and the European Social Charter. It has also ratified the principal United Nations conventions in the field of human rights.

In the Czech Republic, under Article 10 of the Constitution, the provisions of international conventions on human rights take precedence over provisions of internal law and are directly applicable.

Civil and Political Rights

There is adequate opportunity for access to the courts in the Czech Republic. A system of legal aid exists for criminal cases and also, in certain instances, for civil actions.

The death penalty was abolished for all offences in 1990 and is prohibited by the Constitution.

There is protection against arbitrary arrest, such that a person may not be arrested without a warrant issued by the Prosecutor's Office and must be brought before a judge within 24 hours. Within the following 24 hours, the judge will decide if the person is to be released or charged. However, periods of remand have tended to increase in length over recent years (average of 89 days in 1989 compared with 200 in 1995).

Electoral rights are guaranteed for all citizens aged 18 years or over.

Freedom of association is guaranteed in the Czech Republic, as demonstrated by the existence of a large number of active bodies (33 000 associations and 4 700 foundations). They enjoy tax advantages (30% tax reduction) but not total relief in respect of their activities.

Freedom of assembly is only restricted for reasons concerning protection of the rights and freedoms of other persons or on grounds of public order, morality, health or State security. The Constitution also permits a ban on demonstrations potentially prejudicial to the 'prosperity of the country'. However, to date, there is no record of this provision having been applied.

Freedom of expression is evident in the pluralism of the media, both in the press and the audio-visual sector with 11 national daily newspapers, 4 television channels (2 public and 2 private), some 60 radio stations, and numerous foreign channels carried by the cable network). However, freedom of expression is limited under the Criminal Code, which prescribes sentences of up to 2 years' imprisonment for defamation of the Republic and its President. So far, these rules have not had excessively harsh consequences since the President of the Republic has generally pardoned those liable for such penalties. Likewise, it was deemed by the Constitutional Court in 1994 that these rules did not apply to defamation of Parliament, the Government or the Court itself.

Another difficulty is that some of the laws governing this sector are outdated. For example, the press continues to be subject to a law of 1966, and although amendments made between 1990 and 1992 improved the protection of journalists' sources of information, they failed to deal adequately with journalists' access to administrative documents. The audio-visual sector too is still subject to laws adopted in 1991, prior to the establishment of the first private channels.

Ownership rights are guaranteed and expropriation is possible only on grounds of public utility and subject to adequate compensation. However, restitution of expropriated property applies only to confiscation imposed after 25 February 1948 and may benefit Czech citizens only. The person concerned may choose between restitution of the asset or financial compensation calculated according to criteria laid down by law. The Constitutional Court ruled in 1996 that residence in the Czech Republic should not be a requirement for entitlement to benefit under the law on restitution. There is currently a dispute about assessment of the number of buildings and hectares of woodland to be returned to the Catholic Church. The Czech authorities are working on computerisation and updating of the land register.

Respect for privacy is assured: a warrant must be issued by a judge before any police search or phone tapping may take place.

The question of acquisition has posed problems. At the time of partition, the Czech Republic demanded that Slovaks resident on its territory be able to show a clean police record over the previous five years in order to qualify for naturalisation. The move, which deprived a number of gypsies (Roma) of Czech nationality, was inconsistent with the rule that state succession cannot result in people who have lived continuously in the territory becoming aliens or stateless persons; it was relaxed by a law introduced in April 1996 which exempted persons resident on Czech soil on 31 December 1992, subject to possession of a clean police record over the previous five years.

The Czech Republic has ratified the Geneva Convention on Refugees, thereby giving asylum seekers internationally guaranteed rights and protection.

There have been no reported cases of inhuman or degrading treatment.

Economic, Social and Cultural Rights

The right to a minimum means of subsistence and social security are enshrined in the Charter of Fundamental Rights, itself incorporated in the Constitution.

Freedom to engage in trade union activity is a guaranteed right in the Czech Republic. There are some 57 trade unions, most of which are grouped within two large confederations. The rate of union membership is approximately 60%.

The right to strike is recognised, with the exception of judges and personnel of the armed and security forces.

Freedom of education and religion are also guaranteed rights; 21 religious denominations are registered and receive State financial aid if they number at least 10 000 members. The Jewish community benefited from these provisions from 1989, before that threshold was set.

A law was introduced in 1992 to combat racism, anti-semitism and incitement to racial hatred. These legal measures were strengthened in 1995 with stiffer penalties imposed to curb such actions.

Minority Rights and the Protection of Minorities

Minorities in the Czech Republic account for approximately 7% of the population, mainly Slovaks (4%) and gypsies (Roma) (2%-3% according to various estimates).

International conventions guarantee the protection of minorities. The Czech Republic has not ratified the Council of Europe Framework Convention on National Minorities. Moreover, Recommendation 1201 of the Council of Europe's Parliamentary Assembly, which provides for recognition of the collective rights of minorities, is not legally binding.

The Charter of Fundamental Rights recognises the right of minorities to maintain their own identity, to be educated in their own language and to use that language in their contacts with administrative authorities. There are no specific rules to ensure the representation of minorities in Parliament. All minorities are represented in the Council of Minorities set up in 1992 which is consulted by the Government on all matters pertaining to them. Likewise, each Chamber has a standing committee on human rights and minority rights.

Since partition, Slovaks who have chosen to remain in the Czech Republic have encountered no special difficulties in living there.

The situation with regard to the Roma, however, would appear much more difficult. They are the target of numerous forms of discrimination in their daily lives and suffer particular violence from skinheads, without adequate protection from the authorities or the police. Their social situation is often difficult (though sociological factors to some extent account for this) alongside any discrimination they may suffer from the rest of the population, notably over access to jobs or housing. In addition, the way in which some Roma were expelled during partition has been criticised by a number of humanitarian organisations. A better knowledge of the social situation of the Roma (level of unemployment, health indicators, level of education, etc.) would make it easier to the appropriate decisions.

The already substantial efforts of the Czech authorities in the cultural sphere (e.g. Czech language courses for the Roma population on public radio and television stations, and the financ-

1.3. General Evaluation

The Czech Republic's political institutions function properly and in conditions of stability. They respect the limits on their competences and cooperate with each other. Legislative elections in 1992 and 1996 were free and fair. The opposition plays a normal part in the operation of the institutions. Efforts to improve the operation of the judiciary and to intensify the fight against corruption must be sustained.

There are no major problems over respect for fundamental rights. There are, however, some weaknesses in laws governing freedom of the press. Particular attention will need to be paid to the conditions governing any further extension of a law excluding from public service members of the former security service and active members of the Communist regime. There is a problem of discrimination affecting the Roma, notably through the operation of the citizenship law.

The Czech Republic presents the characteristics of a democracy, with stable institutions guaranteeing the rule of law, human rights, and respect for and protection of minorities.

2. Economic Criteria

In examining the economic situation and prospects of the Czech Republic, the Commission's approach is guided in particular by the conclusions of the European Council in Copenhagen in June 1993, which stated that membership of the Union requires 'the existence of a functioning market economy, as well as the capacity to cope with competitive pressure and market forces within the Union'.

This part of the Opinion therefore gives a concise survey of the economic situation and background, followed by a review of the Czech Republic's progress in key areas of economic transformation (liberalisation of the price and trade system, stabilisation of the economy, structural change, reform of the financial sector) as well as its economic and social development. It concludes with a general evaluation of the Czech Republic in relation to the criteria mentioned by the European Council and a review of prospects and priorities for further reform.

2.1. Economic Situation

Background

The Czech Republic, with a population of 10,3 million, has a gross domestic product (GDP) of 94 billion ECU (expressed in purchasing power parity); its population is about 3% of that of the Union, while its economy is only about 1,4% of that of the Union. GDP per head is about 55% of the Union average. The average monthly wage is 290 ECU a month (October 1996).

The Czech Republic was a founding member of the WTO and of CEFTA; it joined the OECD in 1996.

Progress in Economic Transformation

Czechoslovakia in 1938 was one of the richer countries in Europe, with the majority of the wealth concentrated in what is now the Czech Republic. After the communist take-over in 1948, central planning was imposed. Macroeconomic policies however remained prudent, avoiding the significant imbalances that were visible elsewhere in eastern Europe: little debt was built up and inflationary pressures were relatively subdued. However, by 1989, after 50 years of central planning, it had dropped behind even the least developed Member States.

Reforms began shortly after the fall of the communist regime during the 'velvet revolution' in November 1989. The basic elements were price and trade liberalisation, reduced subsidies to enterprises, internal currency convertibility, restrictive monetary and fiscal policy, institutional changes, and a rapid and comprehensive privatisation programme. While the split into Czech and Slovak Republics in 1993 caused some disruption, the establishment of a market economy continued apace.

In contrast with many other transition economies, privatisation of state-owned enterprises took place relatively early in the transition process. Large parts of state assets were quickly sold off, or distributed among the population under the mass privatisation scheme by vouchers which began in 1992 and was completed in 1994. Restructuring was expected to take place once enterprises were in private hands. This radical privatisation drive led to a dramatic increase in the role of the private sector: from being almost non-existent on the eve of reform, it has grown rapidly and now accounts for an estimated three quarters of output. However, the State still has a majority or significant stake in a number of large enterprises and, most importantly, in the four main banks.

Foreign Direct Investment

Foreign direct investment has been strong in the Czech Republic: the cumulative total for 1989-1996 is estimated at 5,3 billion ECU (source: EBRD). The largest share of FDI came from Germany followed by the Netherlands, and the United States. In 1995, it was particularly high as a result of the investment by a Dutch-Swiss consortium into the telecommunications industry. In 1996, inflows of foreign direct investment totalled 0,96 billion ECU which is 94 ECU per head.

Economic Structure

The economy has the structure of an industrialised nation. *Agriculture* accounts for 5,2% of gross value added (1995), and for some 6,3% of employment. The privatisation process is almost complete. The initial decrease in production was reversed in 1995. Price support is limited but export subsidies are used for certain commodities.

Industry has long had an important part to play in the Czech Republic. The country was successful in producing diverse products from the large-scale production of steel to relatively sophisticated engineering and high quality glass. Under the previous regime, there was overemployment in industry. This is still visible to some extent, as it accounts for 43% of employment, but only 34% of gross value added. The number of redundancies has been relatively limited, but this is increasing in certain areas, for example the steel industry. The economy's energy consumption is very high, which accentuates the impact of price adjustments. Russia will continue to supply the majority of oil and gas

Main indicators of economic structure

(All data for 1996 unless otherwise indicated)

Population	*in million*	10,3
GDP per head	*in PPS-ECU (1995)*	9 410
as % of EU-15 average	*in per cent (1995)*	55
share of agriculture in:		
— gross value added	*in per cent (1995)*	5,2
— employment	*in per cent (1995)*	6,3
Gross foreign debt/GDP	*in per cent*	39
Exports of goods and services/GDP	*in per cent*	57
Stock of foreign direct investment ([1])	*in billion ECU*	5,3
	ECU per head	520

Source: Commission services, national sources, EBRD.
([1]) FDI stock converted at end 1996 exchange rate of 1 ECU = $1,25299.

in the coming years, although the Czech government is successfully diversifying energy sources.

The *services* sector has seen growth for a number of years, in particular through the development of new private activity. As a result, the share of services in output and employment is quite important: it accounted for 53% of gross value added and 50% of employment in 1995. The main growth area has been tourism.

Liberalisation

Price Regime

In 1991, the vast majority of consumer prices were liberalised. By 1995 only prices of energy (gas, electricity, and heating), some public services (health care, transport, communications, water) and housing were administered. They form a relatively high proportion of household consumption, so the weight of the administered prices in the price index is quite significant. At their current level, administered prices do not fully reflect the costs of production. The government is aware of the need to adjust regulated prices. In 1997 significant increases are planned for household rents and energy (as a result of VAT increasing to 22%).

Subsidies have been reduced substantially since 1989 and are now quite low: around 2,5% of GDP. In addition they have generally been applied in a non-discriminatory fashion, and have been designed to avoid interference with market forces and the competitive environment as much as possible. This is particularly true of agriculture.

Trade Regime

The Czech Republic moved rapidly towards a liberal trade regime from the start, on the grounds that this promotes structural adjustment, competition and efficient resource allocation. Many of the old barriers to trade were removed and the remaining ones were made more transparent by transforming them into tariffs. Import tariffs currently average about 5% in weighted value terms — they range from 4% on primary goods to 10% on finished goods. The tariffs are generally applied uniformly.

However, in April 1997, the Czech Government introduced an import deposit scheme as one element of a package of measures to tackle a growing trade deficit, a large budget deficit and a slowdown in growth. The measure requires importers of consumer goods and foodstuffs to deposit 20% of the value of the import in a bank for 180 days. Although the cost increasing effect of the measure is limited, the measure can effectively block all imports by small importers that do not have sufficient access to the financial markets to finance the deposit. Consequently, the exact effect of the measure on the trade deficit is hard to predict. Nevertheless it is clear that this move is a step backwards.

There are measures to support and promote exports based on an Act of 1995. The state support is mainly in the form of export credit guarantees. Two state institutions, the Czech Export Bank and the Export Guarantee and Insurance Corporation, administer the support. In addition, information centres, trade fairs and exhibitions are subsidised by the state. Export licences are still in use, though mainly for surveillance purpose rather than as a restrictive measure.

Foreign Exchange Regime

The currency was made convertible for all current account transactions in October 1995 when the IMF Article VIII obligations were formally accepted, although they had *de facto* applied for several years. At the same time, capital movements, in particular capital inflows, were liberalised extensively. The main restrictions in place relate to the outflow of capital.

In 1991, as a result of a number of realignments the currency was devalued by 75%. It was then fixed against a basket of currencies. The basket changed on a number of occasions, but the exchange rate was effectively fixed within a very narrow band (±0,5%) for over 5 years. The stability of the currency over this period is all the more remarkable given the initial low level of reserves, and the fact that inflation eroded the competitive advantage of the 1991 devaluation.

The currency's stability was helped greatly by the fact that the Czech National Bank has total and exclusive control of the exchange rate. In recent years, a somewhat paradoxical situation developed. On the one hand, the positive economic developments attracted very considerable capital inflows — both in the form of direct investment and short-term capital inflows, attracted by the combination of high interest rates and a very solid exchange rate. This tended to strengthen the currency. In contrast, the existence of a huge trade deficit suggested the currency might need to be devalued to maintain export competitiveness. In the event the Bank opted to widen the crown's fluctuation bands to ±7,5% from February 1996, introducing an element of uncertainty that would deter speculative inflows, and give monetary policy more autonomy. The move was successful in that the short-term flows dropped sharply.

In 1996 and early 1997, the currency continued to remain strong despite a soaring current account deficit which was no longer fully financed by capital inflows. However strong pressure for a devaluation in the currency started to emerge during April, developing into a currency crisis in the middle of May 1997. Nervous sentiment on the foreign exchange markets about emerging markets with large current account deficits generally, combined with domestic political instability, resulted in attacks on the currency. The Czech National Bank did initially attempt to support the currency, but on May 27, it was forced to abandon the currency band and to allow the currency to float. The abandoning of the exchange rate regime allowed the currency to depreciate significantly: the crown depreciated by over 20% against the dollar, and over 7% against the mark over levels at the end of 1996.

It is necessary to wait and see at what rate the currency stabilises before it can be seen how the economy will react to the large devaluation. However the devaluation is likely to increase inflation temporarily, somewhat postponing convergence with inflation rates in the EU. It should also increase exports, providing spare capacity can be mobilised to meet the increase in demand.

Stabilisation of the Economy

Domestic

The Czech Republic has been successful in achieving macroeconomic stabilisation, thus laying a firm basis for strong and steady growth. From the outset, the csfr had opted for tight monetary and fiscal policies. These were combined with a sharp competitive devaluation. This gave the economy, and in particular exports, a cushion by making goods very competitive internationally. Exporters were not penalised by domestic inflation, which unavoidably remained relatively high for some time as prices were freed and subsidies removed. After the initial devaluation the exchange rate was fixed to avoid importing further inflation. These policies were adhered to strictly, and were continued after the split of the federation. They began to produce dividends in 1994 when economic growth resumed, as a result of strong exports and very rapid investment, and inflation came down to 10%.

By the end of 1995 the economic situation was strong: single-digit inflation, low unemployment, a budget surplus, increasing household incomes and rapid investment. Economic activity was increasing steadily: agriculture recovered and industry was very dynamic. However, in 1996 growth, though still solid, slowed, unemployment rose, inflationary pressure persisted, a deficit on the budget emerged and the current account deficit soared to 8% of GDP. The deterioration has been attributed to the lack of restructuring, a shortage of skilled labour and the fact that corporate governance is not always totally effective.

In April 1997, the Czech government announced a package of measures aimed at boosting economic growth and tackling the problems of growing budget and trade deficits. The measures included budget cuts, limits on public sector wage growth, lowering corporate taxes, raising certain excise duties and the introduction of an import deposit programme. On 28 May 1997, after the Czech National Bank was forced to abandon the exchange rate band, the government announced a further package of measures. This second package reinforced the government's commitment to the policies announced in April, but also included further cutbacks in state expenditure, and a ban on imports financed through the government budget. It is too early to know the impact of these two sets of measures. The government has warned that if the external position does not improve significantly by the third quarter of 1997, it may consider taking further restrictive trade measures such as introducing an import surcharge.

External

The Czech Republic is an open economy, with exports of goods accounting for 37% of GDP. Trade remained very dynamic for several years. Although the overall position is still strong, imbalances are evident.

The trade deficit has been increasing: it reached 4,6 billion ECU (11% of GDP) in 1996, and was 1,3 billion ECU for the first quarter of 1997. Although a deficit is to be expected in a rapidly growing economy, the current level is particularly high, and there is a limit to the economy's ability to finance it in spite of high tourist receipts. As a result, there is a current account deficit, which reached 3,5 billion ECU in 1996. In 1995, when a large current account deficit first emerged, it was fully financed by very large capital inflows. However, in 1996, this was no longer the case: as a result foreign exchange reserves fell by over 1,2 billion ECU in the year. Reserves remained reasonably strong in the first part of 1997, at the end of March they stood at 10,2 billion ECU, but it is estimated that up to 2,6 billion ECU of these were used by the Czech National Bank to defend the currency when it came under attack in May 1997.

The external debt of the Czech Republic is moderate and represents less than 40% of GDP. The majority of it is medium and long term debt and the debt service is equivalent to under 15% of exports of goods and services.

Structural Change

Foreign Trade

As with other countries in the region, there has been a re-orientation of trade away from Eastern Europe and towards the EU. Since the Czech Republic became an independent nation at the beginning of 1993, the value of its trade with the EU has risen substantially, and the EU is now the country's main trading partner: in 1996 the EU accounted for 59% of Czech exports and 63% of imports.

The goods traded are also highly concentrated. Two categories accounted for more than half of all exports: machinery and transport equipment accounted for 33% and manufactured goods accounted for 29%. In 1996, exports of manufactured goods actually contracted, having been one of the main growth areas before. Apart from a temporary weakening of demand in the EU, this may reflect either a fall in competitiveness or a lack of capacity to produce. The same two categories are the most important for imports as well: machinery 38% and manufactured goods 19%. The main growth area was beverages but this is closely followed by fuels.

The re-orientation of trade and the ability of Czech exports to penetrate new markets suggests that the quality of goods has been improving. However, the value-added of the goods

Main economic trends

		1994	1995	1996
Real GDP growth rate	*in per cent*	2,6	4,8	4,0
Inflation rate:				
— Annual average	*in per cent*	10,0	9,1	8,8
— December on December	*in per cent*	9,7	7,9	8,6
Unemployment rate, end-year	*in per cent* *ILO définition*	3,8	3,6	3,4
General government budget balance	*in per cent of GDP*	1,0	0,6	0,0
Current account balance	*in per cent of GDP*	−0,1	−2,9	−8,6
Debt/export ratio	*in per cent*	51,3	59,1	69,3
Foreign direct investment	*in per cent of GDP*	2,1	5,5	2,4

Source: Commission services, national sources, EBRD

exported to the West is relatively low. The competitive advantage of the Czech Republic certainly comes from low wages and a highly qualified labour force. Before the recent depreciation of the currency this had been largely eroded by high wage growth. Productivity gains and quality improvements will become increasingly important if the Czech Republic is to maintain its markets over the medium term.

The economy is open: exports plus imports of goods and services account for 107% of GDP. Exports have been growing steadily, despite the real appreciation of the currency and the rising unit labour costs. However, the pattern, composition and extent of trade make the Czech Republic very vulnerable to external shocks. For example, it is dependent on energy imports — particularly oil.

Labour Market

One of the most remarkable features of the transition in the Czech Republic, which sets it apart from all other countries in the region, is that it has suffered virtually no unemployment. Unemployment initially rose as a result of transition, but it only reached 5% at its highest point and remained around 3% from early 1995 to the end of 1996. The main reasons for this were that many working pensioners withdrew from the labour force, and that employment opportunities in the private sector developed rapidly. There is still overstaffing, especially in the remnants of old state industry and the public sector, including the railways, which has also contributed to keeping unemployment down. At the beginning of 1997, unemployment increased to over 4% and looks set to rise further as lay-offs have been increasing in certain industries, e.g., steel. However, it remains low relative to most other European countries.

The labour market is very tight and there is said to be a shortage of skilled labour, as a result, wage pressure is high. Until July 1995, with the agreement of the unions, there was an explicit incomes policy — an excess-wage tax — which sought to limit real wage growth to a maximum of 5% above productivity growth. However, it appeared to have counter-productive effects — the maximum was used as the norm — and it was thus abolished. There was no surge in wage demands after it, which suggests it did not artificially contain increases. The fact that real wage growth is above productivity growth is one of the main sources of concern for macroeconomic policy because it contributes to inflationary pressure, by increasing producer costs and boosting consumer demand. In 1996, wages grew by 8,5% in real terms, compared to overall productivity growth of 4%.

There is a minimum wage. In January 1996 it was set at 2 500 crowns per month (based on a $42^1/_2$-hour week), which was then 27% of the average wage. The nominal value is being deliberately capped so that, as inflation persists, its real value will be eroded. The wage distribution is still much narrower than in current Member States.

The payroll tax, which was used to fund unemployment and pension benefits under command planning, was removed in 1993 and replaced with social security contributions. These also cover state employment policies, social assistance and sickness insurance, and are consolidated into the state budget. Health care is separated from the state budget and is run as a funded insurance system, rather than on a pay-as-you-go basis.

Employers' federations and unions exist, but they do not appear to play a very dominant role in areas of macroeconomic importance, such as wage setting.

Public Finances

The role of the state had to change significantly when central planning was abandoned. To support the new role of government, fundamental fiscal reform was required. On the expenditure side, this began in 1990 with a reduction in current transfers to enterprises and households. On the revenue side it took place mainly in January 1993 when value-added tax, personal income tax and corporate profits tax were introduced and/or streamlined.

As a result of the reforms, both the size and the structure of the budget have changed. The importance of indirect taxation has increased, and government expenditure as a percentage of GDP has been reduced to below the levels prevailing in most EU Member States. The guiding principles for fiscal policy have been to balance the budget and to reduce the share of expenditure in GDP; this means that fiscal policy is not used actively to affect the macroeconomics situation. Up until 1996, the Czech

Republic ran surpluses on the state budget. However, in 1996, a shortfall in revenue led to a very small deficit despite the emergency cuts in investment implemented during the year.

There are separate budgets for the state, municipalities and the various funds providing social security. To contain costs, the general income support for the economically active population was abolished in 1993 and unemployment benefits were trimmed. Social security is financed through employer and employee contributions (26% and 8% respectively of the gross wage).

Enterprise Sector: Privatisation and Enterprise Restructuring

The move to a market economy is clearly intimately linked with privatisation of state-owned property and the restructuring of the production processes. The privatisation process in the Czech Republic has been rapid and comprehensive. Privatisation of small state-owned enterprises took place in 1991/1992. Large enterprises have been sold off under the mass privatisation programme which took place in two waves: 1992/1993 and 1994/1995. The majority of the vouchers for the mass privatisation distributed to individuals were placed with investment funds which then bought up the shares. As a result, the role of the investment funds in firms' management is extensive. Since the investment funds are largely owned by banks, there are questions over the ability of the funds to manage companies objectively — there are potential conflicts of interest as banks are both owners and creditors. In addition, bankruptcies tend to propagate more rapidly because of the existence of such links: there was indeed a series of failures across banks and investment funds in 1996 and in early 1997. The main assets yet to be privatised are the main state-owned banks and the utilities.

Industrial production has diversified since 1990 but it is still dominated by metal production. Although small enterprises have increased their share of the market, large firms dominate: in 1995, 81% of output was produced by large firms (with over 100 employees) and 20% by very large firms (with over 5000 employees). The most dynamic enterprises are the very small and the very large; medium-sized firms with 100-5000 employees are below average. There is no evidence on the profitability of firms but there is some concern that only firms with foreign ownership have been investing. In 1995 most investment went to telecommunications and the banking sector, rather than manufacturing.

Productivity growth and restructuring are crucial if production is to become efficient and able to cope with competition. The speed of restructuring depends in part on the access to new investment. Investment finance can come from retained earnings or from domestic borrowing, from sales of shares or brought in from abroad. Investment in general has been strong but this has mostly come from government and gone to infrastructure projects, as has a large proportion of the FDI. Corporate restructuring needs to progress further. Productivity growth has been relatively slow considering the share of investment in GDP and the low rate of unemployment. Also, corporate governance is still not sufficiently strong, partly as a result of the method of privatisation used. Further, since 1996 strikes and protests by workers, including railway and other public sector workers, have taken place against restructuring plans.

Financial Sector

The authority responsible for monetary policy is the Czech National Bank (CNB) which was created on 1 January 1993, taking over from its federal predecessor. Its main objective was to ensure stability of the national currency. It was made independent from the government, but is accountable to Parliament. Its independence is guaranteed by the Act on the CNB and by the Czech Constitution. The CNB does not set targets for inflation, but has a target range for money supply growth. Although inflation has come down and the currency remained stable, the targets for money have generally been missed.

The two-tier banking system, in which the central bank is separated from commercial banking, was well established by 1993. Initially, the main instrument of monetary policy was quantity limits on the amounts banks could lend and borrow. The use of indirect instruments, such as open-market operations (treasury bills and bank bills) and regulation (e.g., setting minimum reserve requirements, discount and Lombard rates), to manage the money supply and the exchange rate became common only gradually after 1993.

The formal reform of the banking sector is essentially complete, but further restructuring is both necessary and expected. State participation accounted for 31,5% of banks' capital by the end of 1995. Domestic banks accounted for 91,5% of deposits at the end of 1995; banks with state participation accounted for about 70% of total bank assets. Banks only fulfil their role of financial intermediation to a limited extent, and there are problems facing the sector at present. Firstly, there are too many small banks that are inefficient and therefore will not be able to survive as they are. During 1996, the rate at which banks ran into problems increased. Secondly, there is a significant amount of inter-ownership of banks and cross-ownership between investment funds and banks. Finally, the bad loans problem for banks, though it has improved, is still present. There are still wide spreads between interest rates on credits and on deposits. At present, therefore, the banking system cannot be considered sufficiently efficient or able to compete, but the system is stable: 80% of banking business is concentrated in the four main state-owned banks, and they currently are relatively healthy. As a result of the unease in the sector, the government is concentrating on privatising each of the main four banks, one at a time.

The capital market, in particular the Prague stock exchange, has developed partly because of mass privatisation. The basic legal and institutional frameworks have been set up. It is the largest stock exchange in the region, by number of stocks and capitalisation, but trading has not increased rapidly, probably because the market lacks transparency. The stock exchange is not yet a significant way of raising finance for enterprises. The capital markets have been criticised by observers and investors for being poorly regulated and confusingly complicated. Illegal activity was discovered in some investment funds. In addition, there currently exist multiple markets for the trading of shares and securities, so that several prices can prevail for the same stocks. In response to these criticisms, considerable changes in the rules of the stock exchange, aimed at enhancing investor protection and market transparency, were introduced in July 1996. Also, the Ministry of Finance aims to set up an independent Securities Commission to improve supervision and regulation of the financial markets, as well as a clearing house to centralise the activity of the multiple markets. The governing body of the Stock Exchange has also proposed tackling the transparency problem by increasing reporting of financial results, and by limiting the number of markets on which stocks can be simultaneously quoted.

The insurance market is still under-developed but competition is increasing.

Economic and Social Development

Social Indicators

The Czech Republic has a population of 10,3 million. As with many countries the population is ageing: birth rates are low and life expectancy is increasing. Some 60% of the population is of working age. This is set to increase slightly in the short to medium term as the retirement age is raised.

In general, there has always been broad consensus on reforms and little social unrest. However, in 1996 and early 1997 a number of strikes was held in the public sector.

The labour force is skilled and educated: in 1995, 32% of the employed had higher secondary education, including vocational training. In addition, 40% had apprenticeship qualifications and a further 11% had university education. The educational system produces a high percentage of science and engineering graduates.

Regional and Sectoral Differences

The various regions of the Czech Republic were formerly fairly homogenous but, since the 'velvet revolution', have begun to show increasing heterogeneity in terms of unemployment rates, wages and inflation.

Prague has developed more rapidly than any other area, and its economy is showing signs of overheating: very low unemployment, and high and rising costs both in terms of wages and rents. Meanwhile the fortunes of other regions have depended largely on the existing industrial base and on whether they could expand tourism and/or exploit proximity to Germany and Austria and the capital.

Under the former regime there was an excessive concentration of industry, so that not only were firms very large but also, due to specialisation, the areas were sensitive to changes in the fortunes of that industry. Northern Bohemia and Northern Moravia are the industrial heartland. Employment has changed little, suggesting there is still a substantial amount of restructuring to be undertaken. Nevertheless, in November 1996, they had the highest unemployment rates at 7,2% and 6% respectively (compared to Prague at 0,4% and the national average of 3,3%). The Southern regions, although dominated by agriculture, have developed their tourist industry significantly and therefore have kept unemployment rates down to 2-3%.

The aim of the regional policy now being developed will be to redress imbalances and facilitate development in less favoured regions. It will aim also to enhance growth by preventing the over-concentration of activity and thus limit congestion and pollution.

2.2. The Economy in the Perspective of Membership

Introduction

The European Council in Copenhagen in 1993 defined the conditions that the associated countries in Central and Eastern Europe need to satisfy for accession. The economic criteria are:

☐ the existence of a functioning market economy;

☐ the capacity to cope with competitive pressure and market forces within the Union.

These criteria are linked. Firstly, a functioning market economy will be better able to cope with competitive pressure. Secondly, in the context of membership of the Union, the functioning market is the internal market. Without integration into the internal market, EU membership would lose its economic meaning, both for the Czech Republic and for its partners.

The adoption of the *acquis,* and in particular the internal market *acquis,* is therefore essential for a candidate country, which must commit itself permanently to the economic obligations of membership. This irreversible commitment is needed to provide the certainty that every part of the enlarged EU market will continue to operate by common rules.

The capacity to take on the *acquis* has several dimensions. On the one hand, the Czech Republic needs to be capable of taking on the economic obligations of membership, in such a way that the Single Market functions smoothly and fairly. On the other hand, the Czech Republic's capacity to benefit fully from the competitive pressures of the internal market requires that the underlying economic environment be favourable, and that the Czech economy have flexibility and a sufficient level of human and physical capital, especially infrastructure. In their absence, competitive pressures are likely to be considered too intense by some sections of society, and there will be a call for protective measures, which, if implemented, would undermine the Single Market.

The capacity and determination of a candidate country to adopt and implement the *acquis* will be crucial, since the costs and benefits of doing so may be unevenly spread across time, industries and social groups. The existence of a broad based consensus about the nature of the changes to economic policy which membership of the Union requires, and a sustained record of implementation of economic reforms in the face of interest group pressure reduce the risk that a country will be unable to maintain its commitment to the economic obligations of membership.

At the level of the public authorities, membership of the Union requires the administrative and legal capacity to transpose and implement the wide range of technical legislation needed to remove obstacles to freedom of movement within the Union and so ensure the working of the Single Market. These aspects are examined in later chapters. At the level of individual firms, the impact on their competitiveness of adopting the *acquis* depends on their capacity to adapt to the new economic environment.

Existence of a Functioning Market Economy

The existence of a market economy requires equilibrium between supply and demand to be established by the free interplay of market forces. A market economy is functioning when the legal system, including the regulation of property rights, is in place and can be enforced. The performance of a market economy is facilitated and improved by macroeconomics stability and a degree of consensus about the essentials of economic policy. A well-developed financial sector and an absence of significant barriers to market entry and exit help to improve the efficiency with which an economy works.

The framework for a functioning market economy is largely in place in the Czech Republic. Market mechanisms dominate: only a minority of administered prices still have to be adjusted, and trade and the foreign exchange regime have been broadly liberalised. Private ownership has been extended, and the privatisation process is almost complete with only the main banks and some 60 strategic enterprises left in state hands. The legal and institutional features of a market system have also largely been adopted: property rights are well-defined; a commercial code has been introduced along with contract and consumer laws; there are no significant administrative controls blocking entry to the market; and the banking sector has been reformed to some extent.

However, it is not clear that all market institutions are as yet sufficiently strong or completely operational. Two main examples are the financial and capital markets, which are an essential feature of a modern market economy, and public administration. These clearly need to develop further. The regulation of the financial markets, which to date has proved inadequate, is under review at present. More specifically, the banking sector is not strong and is undergoing the structural reform necessary for it to fulfil its financial intermediation role effectively. Tax administration has been relatively weak.

Substantial progress has been made in stabilising the economy: inflation is in single digits, unemployment is exceptionally low, and public finances are sound. This has boosted the development of the market system, as it created a stable macroeconomics environment necessary for agents to plan their activity with reasonable certainty. The basis and sustainability of growth appear sound. However, in 1996 economic growth slowed, unemployment and inflation edged up, public finances came under some pressure, the current account deficit soared, and in May 1997 the currency band had to be abandoned. Two factors behind the slowdown were the decline in exports to the Union and tighter monetary policy. The current situation suggests two things. First, that macroeconomics stability cannot be taken for granted, and in particular that ways may need to be found to contain consumer spending so as to limit the size of the trade deficit. Second, that for longer-term solid growth further substantial restructuring at the enterprise level is still needed.

One indicator of how successful the Czech Republic was at adapting and managing its economic development during the first few years of transition, is that it was the first central European country to become a member of the Organisation for Economic Co-operation and Development in 1996. In the coming months continued firm commitment to stabilisation and reform will need to established in order to build upon the substantial progress that the Czech Republic has made in recent years. In addition, good progress in implementation of the Europe Agreement should help to ensure that the transition to membership of the Union is relatively smooth.

Capacity to cope with Competitive Pressure and Market Forces

It is difficult, some years ahead of prospective membership, and before the Czech Republic has adopted and implemented the larger part of Community law, to form a definitive judgement of the country's ability to fulfil this criterion. Nevertheless, it is possible to identify a number of features of the Czech Republic's development which provide some indication of its probable capacity to cope with competitive pressure and market forces within the Union.

This requires a stable macroeconomics framework within which individual economic agents can make decisions in a climate of a reasonable degree of predictability. There must be a sufficient amount of human and physical capital including infrastructure to provide the background so that individual firms have the ability to adapt to face increased competitive pressure in the Single Market. Firms need to invest to improve their efficiency, so that they can both compete at home and take advantage of economies of scale which flow from access to the Single Market. This capacity to adapt will be greater, the more firms have access to investment finance, the better the quality of their workforce, and the more successful they are at innovation.

Moreover, an economy will be better able to take on the obligations of membership the higher the degree of economic integration it achieves with the Union ahead of accession. The more integrated a country already is with the Union, the less the further restructuring implied by membership. The level of economic integration is related to both the range and volume of goods traded with Member States. Direct benefits from access to the Single Market may also be greater in sectors where there are a sizeable proportion of small firms, since these are relatively more affected by impediments to trade.

One indicator of the Czech Republic's competitiveness is its degree of trade integration with the EU. Indeed, the Czech economy has re-oriented its trade toward the West and increased trade turnover dramatically. As a result the economy is quite integrated with the Union: the Union accounts for some 60% of exports and of imports to the Czech Republic. However, they are not currently exporting and importing a similar range of products, which would be an even clearer indicator of competitiveness on the EU market. The structure of trade (using narrow categories of goods) between the Czech Republic and Germany, its main trading partner, shows this and therefore suggests that integration still has some way to go. Given the rising labour costs, further structural changes, productivity growth, and quality improvements are still necessary if Czech firms are to be able to compete with European suppliers.

Another indicator of competitiveness is the ability of enterprises to adjust to changed circumstances and for managers to restructure enterprises and adopt internationally accepted norms and practices. For example, in order to meet technical norms implied by the *acquis,* firms may need to be able to adopt modern technologies. The indirect evidence of restructuring has been mixed so far. The weak management capablility of industry has an important negative effect on industry competitiveness. The number of redundancies in the past has been relatively limited, suggesting that working practices may not have changed and there may still be overstaffing. There are signs, from the steel industry for example, that this is beginning to change, but in other areas such as the railways resistance to change is strong. In addition, because the ownership of enterprises is often not transparent, there is no single clear entity to which managers are responsible or accountable, so they are not necessarily always being prompted to restructure the firms. There is a significant amount of inter-ownership across the banks and investment funds, which hold shares in the enterprises to which the banks lend. Banks have built up some bad loans as a result which have not been cancelled because of the links through the investment funds.

Enterprise restructuring also depends on the level of investment and firms' access to capital. The share of investment in GDP is very high, *foreign direct investment* has been relatively strong, and *R & D spending* as a percentage of GDP has been increasing since 1993: it stood at 1,14% in 1995. To date, the majority of the investment has gone to infrastructure and the banking sector, while investment in manufacturing has been relatively weak. There is indirect evidence that this is changing: the amount of *bank lending to firms* has been increasing and *productivity growth* in manufacturing has been accelerating. Increased access to capital can be expected to help Czech industry adapt to the requirements of the *acquis*.

The costs of adjusting to greater competition depends in part on the degree of industrial and enterprise concentration and on labour mobility. In the Czech Republic industrial production is fairly concentrated in metal production but diversity has been increasing and enterprise concentration has been falling. However, labour mobility is very restricted by the lack of housing.

The agricultural sector is relatively small in terms of its share of GDP. However, significant modernisation would be required upon accession. More or less substantial price adjustments could be necessary, depending on price trends in the country as well as in the EU, and on real exchange rate movements.

At present, the *banking sector* is not competitive or strong. The sector has been reformed but is dominated by the four major banks, which are still partly state-owned; a large number of unviable small banks still exist. During 1996, the weaknesses in the bank sector have came to the fore as a number of banks failed. The main problems in the sector are the existence of bad loans, lack of competitiveness, lack of transparency and inter-ownership of banks and investment funds, and, finally, under-capitalisation. The state may have to intervene to solve the problem of bad loans for some banks. For the sector to develop, it needs to consolidate, and for banking practice on lending to improve further. Progress in this area is essential for the Czech economy to achieve the competitiveness required for the European market.

Prospects and Priorities

The main policy debates currently are on the trade deficit, inflation, the exchange rate, enterprise restructuring and banking sector reform. Underlying them are some fundamental problems which will need addressing in the medium term.

A trade deficit is a normal feature of a rapidly developing economy. There is no cause for concern as long as the deficits are generated by productive investment and financed by long-term capital inflows. However, large persistent imbalances across the balance of payments suggest that there are more fundamental problems. Imports still largely consist of investment goods but imports of consumption goods are growing strongly. The problem is therefore likely to be related to the very low domestic savings rate, despite the high wage and non-wage income growth — in other words, the very high propensity to consume rather than to save.

Inflation has been brought down to single digits, but in 1996 it stopped slowing. The two sources of inflationary pressure are rapid wage growth and strong domestic demand, and the recent depreciation of the Czech crown is likely to exacerbate the situation. As there will be further price liberalisation and deregulation, which will boost inflation in the near future, some very firm action is needed to contain the existing pressures. The labour market is clearly very tight. This may be in part because there is hidden unemployment and access to jobs is costly because job information services are still limited. On the other hand, productivity growth has not been as high as one might have expected with such low unemployment. All over-staffing needs to be shaken out and investment in labour-saving technology is necessary. This investment is more likely to take place if real interest rates are lower and bank lending is less restricted. The latter would require better collateral and risk assessment. In turn this requires stronger and more transparent capital markets: they are not a source of finance for enterprises at present, which have to turn to the banking sector for loans.

Bank privatisation and reform are high on the agenda at present; the recent difficulties are largely due to inadequate legislation and supervision, bad practice and cross-ownership between investment funds and banks. It is important for the banking sector to be cleaned up.

The instruments of monetary and fiscal policy have been transformed to be more compatible with a market system. Until recently they were achieving their objectives: a stable currency, a balanced budget and a reduction of government expenditure as a share of GDP. Public finances have been reformed along Western lines: for example, vat and income tax have been introduced. However, tax collection could be strengthened and there are growing deficits on pension and social security funds which will cause problems in the medium term.

The economic policies of the Czech Republic, to date, have not been guided by an elaborated medium-term strategy. Certain guiding principles for policy have been laid down. Firstly, to achieve 'stability of the currency': the central bank has responsibility for ensuring low inflation and a stable exchange rate. Secondly, to reduce the size of government and to set a balanced budget. Thirdly, to create a market economy through the privatisation of state assets and the liberalisation of economic relations.

The ability of the government to implement the strategies and maintain a credible policy course set is less certain than before the June 1996 elections. Therefore action on legislation and implementation may be slower.

Economic policies should now give greater emphasis to microeconomic measures. It may take longer for the impact of these to be felt but they are of paramount importance if stability is to be maintained and competitiveness strengthened.

2.3. General Evaluation

The Czech Republic can be regarded as a functioning market economy. Market mechanisms operate widely and the role of the state in the economy has been completely changed. Substantial success has been achieved in stabilizing the economy. Unemployment is among the lowest in Europe. However, as the recent emergence of macroeconomic imbalances has shown, further progress will need to be made over the next few years, notably in strengthening corporate governance and the financial system.

The Czech Republic should be able to cope with competitive pressure and market forces in the Union in the medium term, provided that change at the enterprise level is accelerated. The country benefits from a trained and skilled workforce, and infrastructure is relatively good. Investment in the economy has been high in recent years, with foreign direct investment also strong. It has successfully reoriented its trade towards the West. However, although the quality of exported goods is improving, their value-added is still low. The banking sector is dominated by a few, partly state-owned banks and its competitive position is not strong. The main challenge for the Czech Republic is to press on with enterprise restructuring in order to improve the medium term performance of the economy, and as a way of redressing the external imbalances.

3. Ability to assume the Obligations of Membership

The European Council in Copenhagen included among the criteria for accession 'the ability to take on the obligations of membership, including adherence to the aims of political, economic and monetary union'.

In applying for membership on the basis of the Treaty, the Czech Republic has accepted without reserve the basic aims of the Union, including its policies and instruments. The chapter examines the Czech Republic's capacity to assume the obligations of member — that is, the legal and institutional framework, known as the *acquis*, by means of which the Union puts into effect its objectives.

With the development of the Union, the *acquis* has become progressively more onerous, and presents a greater challenge for future accessions than was the case in the past. The ability of the Czech Republic to implement the *acquis* will be central to its capacity to function successfully within the Union.

The following sections examine, for each main field of the Union's activity, the current and prospective situation of the Czech Republic. The starting-point of the description and analysis is a brief summary of the *acquis*, with a mention of the provisions of the Europe Agreement and the White Paper, where they are relevant. Finally, for each field of activity there is a brief assessment of the Czech Republic's ability to assume the obligations of membership on a medium-term horizon.

3.1. Internal Market without Frontiers

Article 7a of the Treaty defines the Union's internal market as an area without internal frontiers in which the free movement of goods, persons, services and capital is ensured. This internal market, central to the integration process, is based on an open-market economy in which competition and economic and social cohesion must play a full part.

Effective implementation of the liberties enshrined in the Treaty requires not only compliance with such important principles as, for example, non-discrimination or mutual recognition of national regulations — as clarified by Court of Justice rulings — but also concomitant, effective application of a series of common specific provisions. These are designed, in particular, to provide safety, public health, environmental and consumer protection, public confidence in the services sector, appropriately qualified persons to practise certain specialist occupations and, where necessary, introduction or coordination of regulatory and monitoring mechanisms; all systematic checks and inspections necessary to ensure correct application of the rules are carried out on the market, not at frontier crossings.

It is important to incorporate Community legislation into national legislation effectively, but even more important to implement it properly in the field, via the appropriate administrative and judicial structures set up in the Member

States and respected by companies. This is an essential precondition for creating the mutual trust indispensable for smooth operation of the internal market.

This chapter must be read in conjunction with, *inter alia*, the chapters on social policy, the environment, consumer protection and sectoral policies.

The Four Freedoms

A step-by-step approach is being taken to absorption of the *acquis* by the candidate countries:

☐ the Association Agreement between the Community, its Member States and the Czech Republic was signed in 1995 and is being ratified. With regard to the four freedoms and approximation of legislation, the Agreement provides, in particular, for immediate or gradual application of a number of obligations, some of them reciprocal, covering, in particular, freedom of establishment, national treatment, free trade, intellectual property and public procurement;

☐ the Commission's 1995 White Paper (COM(95) 163 final), guidelines intended to help the candidate countries prepare for integration into the internal market, gives a closer definition of the legislation concerned. It identifies the 'key measures' with a direct effect on the free movement of goods, services, capital and persons and outlines the conditions necessary in order to operate the legislation, including the legal and organizational structures. Twenty-three areas of Community activity are examined, dividing the measures into two stages, in order of priority, to provide a work programme for the pre-accession phase. The Technical Assistance and Information Exchange Office (TAIEX) was set up with the objective of providing complementary and focused technical assistance in the areas of legislation covered in the White Paper. A legislative database has recently been established by the Office,

☐ the candidate countries will have to implement all the *acquis*. The 'Action Plan for the Single Market' submitted to the Amsterdam European Council gives details of the priority measures necessary to make the Single Market work better between the Fifteen in preparation for introduction of the single currency. This will inevitably entail changes to the *acquis*.

General Framework

Whatever their field of activity, undertakings must be able to operate on the basis of common rules. These are important since they shape the general framework within which economies operate and, hence, the general conditions of competition. They include the rules on competition (on undertakings and state aid) and tax measures discussed elsewhere in this opinion, the opening-up of public works, supply and service contracts, harmonisation of the rules on intellectual property (including the European patent), harmonisation of the rules on company law and accountancy, protection of personal data, transfer of proceedings and recognition of judgments (Article 220 conventions).

Descriptive Summary

Public Procurement is regulated by a 1994 Act which entered into force in 1996. An independent agency, the Office for the Protection of Competition, is in charge of monitoring the public procurement policy.

In the area of protection of *intellectual* and *industrial property rights* the Czech Republic adopted a new Patent Law in 1990, a Trademark Law in 1995, whereas the Copyright Law was slightly amended in 1996. The country is a party to all conventions referred to in Article 67 of the Europe Agreement and submitted an application to accede to the Munich Convention of 1973. The Czech Republic is a member of the Agreement on Trade Related of Intellectual Property Rights (TRIPs).

Company law is mainly governed by the Commercial Code, last amended on 1 July 1996, which brought close to the First and second Directives. A variety of different types of enterprises are recognised under Czech law, including public and private limited companies. Currently some 115 000 companies are registered. They may issue shares and recent legislation has improved shareholder protection. Minimum capital requirements are laid down by law. There is a basic level of protection for creditors. The courts operate a company register which contains all relevant information about each company, which can be freely consulted.

The Accounting Act of 1991 brings Czech *accounting* regulations in line with the Fourth Directive. There are no accounting standards, procedures are given by the Ministry of Finance. Methodological recommendations are issued by the Union of Accountants. Rules on consolidated accounts are given in Ministry declarations.

The right to the *protection of personal data* is enshrined in the Charter of Fundamental Rights and Freedoms and ensured by Act 256/1992 on the Protection of Personal Data as well as a number of sectoral acts. There does not exist an independent control body to supervise compliance.

Current and Prospective Assessment

Czech *procurement legislation* has moved considerably into the direction of the *acquis*. Most of the White Paper Directives are incorporated into Czech law. The Czech authorities themselves admit, however, that full conformity does not exist yet. This is the case for tendering procedures in the utilities sector — which is not yet covered by the legislation — and the existence of preferences and some other discriminatory measures towards non-residents.

Serious efforts have been made to bring public procurement legislation into line with the *acquis*. Although the Czech Law is in general of good quality, a number of gaps continue to exist. In particular, the scope of the law would need to be extended to all the utilities sectors (water, energy, transport and telecommunications). For the time being the Czech Republic maintains a system of domestic preferences as allowed by the Europe Agreement. Firms located in the EU will get equal access only after the expiry of the transition period set out in the Europe Agreement. The Office for the Protection of Economic Competition seems to meet the infrastructure requirement for a correct implementation of legislation. Although it is too soon to adequately judge the effectiveness of the public procurement procedures in practice, the legal remedies system seems to be rapid and effective, and is in line with most of the requirements of the directives.

Further amendments to the Act on public procurement are expected to be in force by 1998-2000, so as to achieve complete harmonisation in the field of public procurement by the date of accession.

Good progress has been made in the adaptation of legislation concerning *industrial property rights* (patents, trademarks, designs).

In *intellectual property rights* (copyrights and neighbouring rights) important gaps have to be filled (for computer programmes, rental and distribution rights and duration of protection of copyrights). The existing Patent Law is intended to be revised in order to ensure total compatibility with the Munich Convention. At the same time the Czech Republic intends to introduce the SPC (supplementary protection certificate) for pharmaceutical products. Border enforcement will be introduced by 1 January 1998. Piracy remains important. Considerable efforts have been made to ensure an appropriate enforcement for industrial property.

As to *company law*, according to the information provided by the Czech Republic, the Commercial Code was amended as of 1 July 1996 to bring it substantially into line with the First and Second Directives, though certain gaps still need to be filled, for example as regards creditor protection. It is understood that the Twelfth Directive has been transposed into Czech law, but there is not yet full compatibility with the Third and Eleventh Directives.

As regards *accounting* the 1991 Act already goes a good distance towards alignment with the Fourth Directive and amendments to the Act which will become effective on 1 January 1999 are expected to result in full conformity. Amendments to the Act on Auditors implementing the Eight Directive will become effective on 1 January 1998. Certain transitional problems are in evidence relating to the implementation in practice of the new rules, including a shortage of qualified accountants and auditors, but these can be solved in the medium term.

The Czech authorities recognise that Czech legislation does not yet sufficiently comply with European standards concerning *data protection*. The Czech Republic is still not a party to Convention 108 of the Council of Europe. It is necessary to establish an independent body responsible for the supervision of the application of the law and to introduce sanctions to be taken vis-à-vis persons making illegal use of data.

As regards civil law, the Czech Republic has recently been invited by the States Parties to the Lugano Convention on jurisdiction and enforcement of judgements in civil and commercial matters to adhere to that Convention. Such development gives a good indication of confidence in the Czech Republic's judicial system.

Conclusion

The Czech Republic has already taken on the most important Directives for the sectors described above. Implementation of the provisions of the Europe Agreement and the White Paper covering the sectors reviewed has generally been good.

Further work is required, notably in the area of public procurement, intellectual property protection and the implementing structures for personal data protection. Efforts of a lesser degree are required in the field of company law, and accounting to bring Czech legislation fully into line with EC legislation. In all these fields, assuming the continuation of the present harmonisation, there should be no major difficulties for approximation in the medium term.

Free Movement of Goods

Free movement of goods can be achieved only by removing measures which restrict trade — not only customs duties and quantitative restrictions but all measures with equivalent, i.e. protectionist, effect, irrespective of whether or not they are specifically aimed at domestic or imported products. Where technical standards are not harmonised, the free movement of goods must be ensured by applying the principle of mutual recognition of national rules and accepting the rule that national specifications should be no more stringent than is required to achieve their legitimate objectives. This rule was established in the *Cassis de Dijon* judgment.

For the purpose of harmonisation, the European Community has developed the 'New Approach' which introduces an approach carefully balanced between government and private autonomous bodies and in which European Community legislation and European standards play a distinct complementary role. Thus, instead of imposing technical solutions, European Community legislation is limited to establishing the essential requirements which products must meet. Products manufactured in accordance with European standards are presumed to meet such essential requirements, but European standards are not the only way to prove such conformity. The 'New Approach' works in conjunction with the 'Global Approach' on product certification which governs the apposition of the 'CE Mark' on the product. For other products such as pharmaceuticals, chemicals, motor vehicles, and food products, European Community directives follow the traditional regulatory pattern of providing fully detailed rules.

The free movement of goods also dictates that a number of Community harmonisation measures be transposed into national law. Implementation of health and safety harmonisation rules is particularly important and requires the establishment of appropriate mechanisms and organisations, both for businesses and the authorities.

Two of the 'horizontal' directives essential to smooth running of the Single Market are the Directive on general product safety and the Directive on liability for defective products. The regulations concerning general product safety are covered in the section on consumer protection.

The rules on agricultural products (compliance with veterinary and plant-health standards) are explained in detail in the section on agriculture.

Descriptive Summary

Levels of tariff protection are low and there are relatively few discriminatory measures still in place. All prices have been liberalised, with the exception of those for public utilities, and household gas, water, electricity prices and rents.The introduction of an import deposit scheme on 21 April 1997 and the planning of restrictive measures for agricultural imports deviate from the free trade approach followed by the government until now. These matters are presented in other parts of the opinion.

The process of approximation of technical legislation to the EU *acquis* has made good progress. The envisaged entry into force on 1 September 1997 of the 'Act on Technical Requirements for Products' should pave the way for the adoption of technical regulations, standards and conformity assessment procedures which are virtually compatible with the EU's New Approach to technical harmonisation and the Global Approach to conformity assessment.

In the major sectors regulatory alignment seems to progress quite satisfactorily: new legislation on foodstuffs has just been adopted; globally compatible draft legislation exists for chemicals; concerning the automotive sector, the Czech Republic is a signatory of the UN-ECE 1958 Agreement and applies more than two thirds of UN-ECE regulations. On pharmaceuticals draft legislation is likely to reflect progress being made in rendering legislation consistent with the EU. The new Law on Medicinal Products, with the necessary application measures, is expected to be in line with the relevant Community *acquis*. It needs to be borne in mind, in any case, that secondary legislation is often necessary in order to implement the general legislative framework.

The Czech Office for Standards, Metrology and Testing (COSMT), a subsidiary body to the Ministry for Trade and Industry, is responsible for standardisation and certification matters.

The co-existence of different functions under the same umbrella body is a feature of the transition towards a new system based on the New Approach. The latter, however, prescribes independent conformity assessment bodies, a compatible accreditation system, and voluntary standardisation.

More than 80 % of EU standards have been implemented into the Czech national standards system and a 100 % implementation rate should be attained by the end of 1997. COSMT, which became a full member of the Comité européen de normalisation (CEN) earlier this year and is an affiliate member of the Comité européen de normalisation électrotechnique (Cenelec), is likely to remain the technical supervisory authority under the new system.

Until recently there were no examples of technical barriers to trade. Earlier this year, however, there have been occasional reports about products originating in the Community and complying with EU standards not being allowed on the Czech market.

Current and Prospective Assessment

The Czech Republic is well advanced in applying the EC rules regarding the free movement of goods. However, market access for products originating in the European Union which are in conformity with EU standards needs to be guaranteed.

Good progress has been made in regard of the safety of industrial products. Work is proceeding on the implementation of the 'Act on the Technical Requirement for Products' and the subsequent implementation of the transposed New Approach directives.

The Czech Office for Standards, Metrology and Testing has a staff which looks sufficient while the technical competence seems assured.

The draft 'Act on Technical Requirements for Products' provides for the privatisation of the state testing bodies within a year. Inspection bodies in the area of standards and technical norms currently fall under different Ministries. The same applies to certification bodies, which are envisaged to be privatised.

The Czech standardisation and certification system looks rather well prepared to comply with the *acquis* within the medium term, on the condition that current efforts are continued. Questions remain, however, about the implementation of market surveillance (legislation and administrative structure); the separation between the regulatory, standardisation and certification functions; the resolution of the issue of professional secrecy for testing laboratories and the exact intentions of Ministries concerning the privatisation of certification bodies). Monitoring of developments seems therefore necessary. This also applies to the quality and staffing of the bodies and institutions competent for the implementation of the relevant legislation, although also here developments are encouraging.

A bill on civil product liability is due to go before Parliament soon and should come into force next January.

In the areas subject to national rules but not covered by Community harmonisation, there is not enough information available to assess whether Community legal principles on the free movement of goods are properly applied in the Czech Republic.

The reporting procedures which form part of the internal-market machinery are not yet operational and so cannot be used in the pre-accession period. The most important instruments in this connection are: Directive 83/189/EEC, requiring governments to report draft national technical standards and regulations; Decision

3052/95/EC on measures derogating from the principle of the free movement of goods; procedures by which complaints can be submitted to the Commission; and Article 177 of the Treaty, enabling Member States to request preliminary rulings in the Court of Justice. It is also hard to assess whether the Czech Republic complies with the principle of mutual recognition; more information is required on its national rules, and on administrative practices, which can affect product sales.

Conclusion

Significant progress has been made. The Czech Republic has progressed very well in the taking on of the *acquis* related to the free movement of goods and has already taken on the most important directives. Implementation of the provisions of the Europe Agreement and the White Paper has generally been good. However, there must be certainty that products conforming to EC standards are allowed onto the Czech market. Developments concerning the safety of industrial products need to be monitored, both concerning legislation and implementing structures. Provided current efforts are maintained, free circulation of goods should be made possible in the medium term.

The Czech authorities should also ensure that, in areas not covered by Community harmonisation, their own national laws do not hinder trade. In particular, they should check that measures are proportionate to their objectives.

Free Movement of Capital

The Europe Agreement establishes the principle of the free movement of capital between the Czech Republic and the EU. This as far as the obligations of the Czech Republic are concerned applies from the entry into force of the Europe Agreement as regards direct investments made by companies already established in the Czech Republic as regards branches or agencies of Community companies (as well as the self employed), gradually during the transitional period. The parties shall consult each other with a view to facilitate the movement of capital between the Community and the Czech Republic in order to promote the objectives of the Agreement (Article 61 of the Europe Agreement).

The White Paper highlights the link between the free movement of capital and the free movement of financial services. It suggests a sequence of capital movements liberalisation, starting from medium and long term capital movements and those linked to commercial operations, to short-term capital.

Descriptive Summary

The Czech Republic has been able to attract a considerable amount of foreign direct investment (FDI) since 1990. The total figure for the period 1990-1996 stands at 5 300 million ECU. This FDI has played a positive role in the restructuring, privatisation and modernisation of Czech industry. In addition, there was significant inflow of foreign capital in the form of bank deposits and portfolio investment. These developments are in part due to the country's liberal policies concerning the movement of capital.

The Foreign Exchange Law in force since 1 October 1995 introduced *current account* convertibility. The same law introduced also extensive liberalisation of *capital movements*.

Following these measures, most of capital inflows have been liberalised. The main restrictions on the inflow of capital concern the acquisition by non-residents of real estate (for purposes other than direct investment) and the admission of foreign securities to the domestic capital and money markets.

In contrast to capital inflows, much wider is the range of restrictions on the outflow of capital. However, among the liberalised outward capital movements are direct investment, acquisition of real estate by residents abroad, commercial credits and personal capital movements.

The capital movements already liberalised by the Czech Republic exceed the obligations undertaken by this country under the Europe Agreement.

Current and Prospective Assessment

According to the Czech authorities, the abolition of the remaining restrictions will be gradual and is expected to be realised within a period of three to five years.

The Foreign Exchange Law already in place enables further liberalisation steps to be taken by adopting governmental decrees and orders of the Minister of Finance and the National Bank, without a need to change the law. However, for the acquisition of domestic real estate by non-residents the law will have to be amended.

Conclusion

The degree of capital movements liberalisation already achieved is very substantial, with liberalisation of inward capital movements much more rapid than outward capital flows. The Czech Republic is expected to be able to eliminate, without major difficulties, the remaining restrictions on the movement of capital in the medium term and assume fully the Community *acquis* in this area.

Free Movement of Services

The basis of the free movement of services is the prohibition of discrimination, in particular on grounds of nationality, and rules on the alignment of divergent national legislation. These rules often concern both the right of establishment, which comes under the heading of the free movement of persons, and the freedom to provide services. Their implementation implies the establishment of administrative structures (banking control boards, audio-visual control authorities, regulatory bodies) and greater cooperation between Member States in the area of enforcement (mutual recognition arrangements).

A substantial amount of the legislation applicable to the free movement of services relates to financial services. It also concerns the problems relating to the opening-up of national markets in the sectors traditionally dominated by monopolies, e.g. telecommunciations and, to a certain extent, energy and transport. These subjects will be dealt with in the sections of the Opinion specifically referring to them.

Descriptive Summary

Based on the mono-bank system until 1989, the *banking sector* of the Czech Republic experienced a high demand for financial services during the transitional period of the division of the former Czechoslovak Republic in 1993. As a consequence, more than 50 new banks were set up. The following three years were a period of consolidation of the banking sector. This stage required in particular to enhance the stability of the two-tier banking sector which had emerged and to secure the implementation of prudential rules and a system of banking supervision. The current stage may be identified as one of adjustments to EU standards, and up-grading of efficiency and competitiveness of the banking sector.

Seven banks are partly owned by the State; five of them are controlled by it and have a share within the banking market of around 70%. Currently, a project for the privatisation of some of the banks partly owned by the State is under preparation.

The conditions under which foreign banks can operate on the Czech market are generally compatible with the First and Second Banking Directives. The requirements for solvency ratios and large exposure are also in line with the *acquis*. Differences with Community legislation exist concerning deposit guarantee schemes, capital adequacy and consolidated supervision. Difficulties in the banking sector over the past few years led to new government initiatives to further consolidate the sector by stricter regulation and privatisation of the four largest, state owned, banks, including increased participation by foreign capital.

Banking supervision lies with a specialised department of the Czech National Bank. New legislation has brought anti-money laundering policy more in line with the Union requirements, but important gaps remain. The responsible policy authority is the Ministry of Finance.

The *Securities* and *Stock Exchange* Act and the Act 248/1992 on investment companies and funds are serious efforts to bring Czech legislation in line with Stage I measures. Approximation of Stage II measures is envisaged within three to four years. Investment activities can be undertaken by companies which have been granted a license by the Ministry of Finance as well as by credit institutions. Foreign companies providing investment services are granted the same rights as domestic firms. Securities issued abroad may be traded on Czech markets provided that the foreign markets on which they are listed are approved by the Ministry of Finance. The financial sector has been playing a key role in the privatisation programme. The heavy involvement of institutional investors in this area together with the large number of transactions carried out off market urge strict provisions with regard to market manipulation. In addition, a wide cross-ownership between banks (heavily exposed to privatised and privatising companies) and institutional investors give rise to conflict of interest which should be addressed by strengthening minority shareholders' rights and disclosure requirements.

A first move in this direction was the adoption of an amendment to the Securities and Stock Exchange Act in April 1996 and the decision in early 1997 to establish a new supervisory authority, which is still not, however, an independent commission since it continues to operate within the Ministry for Finance, with the National Bank playing a minor role.

Serious problems with a number of investment funds in early 1997 seem to have made the authorities more aware of the need for stricter regulation. It is not yet clear to which concrete results this will lead.

The *insurance sector* is regulated by a 1991 act bringing Czech legislation fairly close to Stage I compatibility. Important differences with the *acquis* that remain to be resolved are the deposit requirements, which are far stricter than those applied in the Union, and the continued predominance of the former state insurance monopoly and its monopoly of motor insurance.

The supervisory authority rests with the Ministry of Finance. It has a specialised department.

Current and Prospective Assessment

Progress in adopting the *acquis* in the *banking sector* has been satisfactory. Differences which still need to be overcome relate to the deposit guarantee schemes, capital adequacy and consolidated supervision. It is planned to remove these remaining restrictions and to propose the Stage I and II Directives in 1997/1998.

According to the Government's legislative programme the full transposition of EU laws on banking and banking supervision will be achieved by the year 2000 including acts on cooperation and information exchange with the Commission and other EU Member States and mutual recognition of bank supervisions. The implementation of the new policy of stricter regulation which developments in recent years have shown to be necessary, needs careful monitoring.

As far as *securities* are concerned, the Directives on public offer prospectus, on insider dealing on collective investment, on investment services and on capital adequacy for market risks (as regards non-bank investment companies) are planned to be transposed over the next two years.

The Securities and Investment Funds Acts seem to reflect Stage I measures in the field of securities. Approximation of Stage II measures is envisaged in the medium term. This will imply the adoption of EU standards regarding authorisation conditions and prudential requirements of investment firms as the basis for granting the European passport. It will also result in safer operational conditions for EU investment firms operating in the Czech Republic. Other necessary adaptation of existing legislation concerns the imposition of stricter requirements on managers and shareholders of investment firms and issuers whose securities are offered to the public.

The Securities Supervisory Commission recently established within the Ministry of Finance has to gain experience in its supervisory role.

In the *insurance sector*, the implementation of the Stage I and II directives has not yet been achieved. According to the Government published plans, the main features of the following directives will be transposed into the amendment to the existing insurance law and will become effective as of 31 December 1998: the first directive on insurance other than life assurance, the insurance agents and brokers directive and the tourist assistance directive The following directives will be transposed into a new insurance law: the directive on legal expenses insurance, the second directive on insurance other than life assurance, the second directive on life assurance, the third generation directives; they will become effective in 2002. The various directives on compulsory insurance against civil liability in respect of use of motor vehicles will be transposed in a new specific law in order to become effective in year 2000.

Conclusion

While the Czech Republic has made considerable progress in other economic areas, the situation in the financial sector is not satisfactory.

In the banking field, the very important market share of banks controlled by the State, cast a doubt on the transparency and the free competition in the market. The crisis of the major privatised banks gives the impression that the banking supervision needs to be strengthened.

In the securities field the recent scandals and the difficulties to set up an independent Securities Commission show that the condition of a free, competitive market with adequate supervision are not yet present.

In the insurance field, the delay in the implementation even of the first stage directives has not contributed to the development of a competitive and efficient insurance market.

Free Movement of Persons

The free movement of persons encompasses two concepts with different logical implications in the Treaty. On the one hand, Article 7a in Part One of the Treaty on 'Principles' mentions the concept in connection with the establishment of the internal market and implies that persons are not to be subject to controls when crossing the internal frontiers between the Member States. On the other hand, Article 8a in Part Two of the Treaty on 'Citizenship of the Union' gives every citizen of the Union the individual right to move and reside freely within the territory of the Member States, subject to certain conditions. The abolition of frontier checks must apply to all persons, whatever their nationality, if Article 7a is not to be meaningless. While the rights deriving from Article 8a apply in all Member States, those stemming from Article 7a have never been fully applied throughout the Union.

a) Free Movement of Union Citizens, Freedom of Establishment and Mutual Recognition of Diplomas and Qualifications

The Europe Agreement provides for the non-discriminatory treatment of workers that are legally employed (as well as their families). It covers the possibility of cumulating or transferring social security rights, and encourages Member States to conclude bilateral agreements with the Czech Republic on access to labour markets. During the second phase of the transitional period, the Association Council will examine further ways of improving the movement of workers.

The White Paper considers the legislative requirements in order to achieve a harmonious development of the labour market, whilst simultaneously preventing distortions of competition.

The free movement of workers is one of the fundamental freedoms enshrined in the Treaty; freedom to practise certain professions (e.g. in the legal and health fields) may, however, be subject to certain conditions, such as qualifications. These may be dealt with either through coordination or by applying the principle of mutual recognition.

Freedom of establishment is also guaranteed under the Treaty and covers the economic activity of self-employed persons and companies.

The free choice of place of residence may thus be subject to minimum conditions as to resources and health insurance where the person does not practice a profession in the country concerned.

Descriptive Summary

Generally foreign workers can enter into employment if they have a residence permit and a work permit, which are subject to certain conditions. An employment permit is not required for Slovak citizens on the basis of the treaty concerning reciprocal employment. A foreigner would be refused a work permit in cases where the vacancies can be filled by Czech citizens.

Members of the foreign worker's family obtain a residence permit on condition that the worker ensures material security and housing.

Termination of the foreigner's employment, including unemployment, means termination of the work permit. Nor is the period of validity of the work permit automatically extended in the case of sickness, accident or other impediments. Foreigners working on the basis of an employment permit have no right to be registered as job seekers nor do they get unemployment benefits.

Members of the family of the foreign worker have access to education, although in many cases costs for education are considerably higher than those for Czech citizens.

Progress has been achieved in the taking over of the *acquis* concerning mutual recognition of diplomas and qualifications. Full approximation is expected in the medium term.

Current and Prospective Assessment

The application of the principle of equal treatment to those EU workers already legally residing in the Czech Republic should not be a problem.

In the field of mutual recognition of diplomas and qualifications the Czech republic has already made progress. However, some adaptations are still necessary. The Czech Republic should be able to take up the *acquis* in the medium term. The existing implementing structures seem to be able to enforce the legislation.

Training, where coordinated by directives for seven professions, is rather broadly in line with the *acquis,* but a number of adaptations are still necessary. As regards structures, Ministries and public bodies (professional organisations, public offices and agencies) exist for many professions, but will probably need to be reinforced. Integration in EU associations is progressing for certain professions, for example engineering diplomas meet the minimum European standards.

Conclusion

The necessary structures in this area seem to be in place, but it is not always easy to assess their real effect and enforcement. The Czech Republic is aware of the outstanding issues that need to be resolved with regard to the free movement of persons. From a technical point of view, adaptations of regulations will be necessary in the medium term.

b) Abolition of Checks on Persons at Internal Frontiers

The free movement of persons within the meaning of Article 7a of the EC Treaty, i.e. the abolition of checks on all persons, whatever their nationality, at the internal frontiers has not yet been fully implemented in the Union. Doing away with checks on persons is conditional on the introduction of a large number of accompanying measures, some of which have yet to be approved and implemented by the Member States (see separate section on Justice and Home Affairs). However, that objective has been achieved by a limited number of Member States in accordance with the Schengen Convention (seven Member States already apply it and another six are working towards implementation).

The draft Treaty aims to make that objective easier to achieve within the Union by including a new chapter on freedom, security and justice and incorporating the Schengen *acquis* into the EU.

The Czech Republic has stated its intention to become party to the Schengen Agreement. It has called for institutional and technical cooperation notably in the field of border control to the upgrading and modernisation of which significant financial resources are being devoted.

General Evaluation

1. The Czech Republic's progress in the implementation of legislation relating to the White Paper is summarised in a table in the Annex. According to the table, the Czech Republic considers that by 30 June 1997 it will have adopted national implementing legislation for 417 of the 899 directives and regulations in the White Paper. That figure covers provisions for which the Republic considers it will have adopted implementing legislation, or which it will have checked for compatibility with Community rules, and does not prejudge actual compatibility as such, on which the Commission is not able at this stage to state an opinion.

2. For most of the Single Market areas, especially company and accounting law, and technical rules and standards, the basic Community laws are mostly in place. Most measures have been partly or fully incorporated according to the Czech authorities although the Commission cannot at this stage say whether they comply wholly with Community law. In certain other fields particularly in the financial services sector, there are still considerable shortcomings to be overcome and further efforts need to be made to ensure the *acquis* is fully adopted.

3. Despite the efforts made, real progress in incorporating those legal texts adopted very recently must go hand in hand with practical implementing measures and an effective administrative infrastructure. Some of this infrastruc-

ture works reasonably well (for example, despite the partial alignment of public procurement legislation it must be noted that legal remedies in this field seem to be working satisfactorily). In the field of technical rules and standards, the technical structures needed to implement the 'New Approach' are on the right path. However, major efforts are still required in a number of areas such as financial services, securities, intellectual property protection and protection of personal data.

At this stage, the Commission cannot say how well-equipped businesses, particularly SMEs, are to implement the *acquis*.

4. Leaving aside certain specific aspects relating to agriculture, checks at the internal frontiers of the Union can only be abolished once sufficient legislative harmonisation has been achieved. This calls for mutual confidence, based in particular on sound administration (e.g. the importance of safety checks on some products at the place of departure).

With respect to goods, the completion of the internal market on 1 January 1993 was only achieved by removing all the formalities and checks performed by the Member States at the internal borders of the Union. In particular these checks covered particularly technical points (product safety), veterinary, animal-health and plant-health matters, economic and commercial matters (e.g. prevention of counterfeiting of goods), security (weapons, etc.) and environmental aspects (waste, etc.). In most cases, the abolition of checks was only made possible by the adoption and application of Community measures harmonising the rules on movement and placement on the market (particularly as regards product safety) and, where applicable, by shifting the place where controls and formalities within the Member States or on their markets are conducted (in particular as regards VAT and excise duties, veterinary and plant-health checks, and the collection of statistics). Were the Czech Republic's present borders to become the Union's external frontier, border checks would have to be stepped up (see separate section on customs).

In view of the overall assessment that can be made of progress achieved to date and the rate at which work is advancing in the various areas concerned, there is no reason to believe that the Czech Republic would not in the medium term be able to adopt and implement all the legal acts needed for the abolition of internal border controls or the transfer of these controls to the Union's external frontier.

5. The Czech Republic has already adopted significant elements of the *acquis* relating to the Single Market; however, the Commission is not yet able to take a position on every measure whose transposition has been reported by the Czech Republic. In many areas enforcement needs to be strengthened. Provided that current efforts continue, it can be expected that in the medium term the Czech Republic will have adopted and implemented the legislation, and made the necessary progress on mechanisms of enforcement, in order to be able to participate fully in the Single Market.

Competition

European Community competition policy derives from Article 3 (g) of the Treaty providing that the Community shall have a system ensuring that competition in the internal market is not distorted. The main areas of application are anti-trust and state aid.

The Europe Agreement provides for a competition regime to be applied in trade relations between the Community and the Czech Republic based on the criteria of Articles 85 and 86 of the EC Treaty (agreements between undertakings/abuses of dominant position) and in Article 92 (state aid), and for implementing rules in these fields to be adopted within three years of the entry into force of the Agreement. Furthermore it provides that the Czech Republic will make its legislation compatible with that of the Community in the field of competition.

The White Paper refers to the progressive application of the above provisions and those of the Merger Regulation [(EEC) No 4064/89] and of Article 37 and 90 (Monopolies and Special Rights).

Descriptive Summary

Competition legislation is based on *Act No 63/1991 on the Protection of Economic Competition* and was drafted on the basis of the model of EC competition law. The Czech competition law covers all the different sectors of the economy as well as public and private enterprises.

The Authority responsible for competition policy is the *Office for the Protection of Economic Competition*. Officials from this body have a good general understanding of competition law principles and have gained experience in the antitrust field.

As to *sectors traditionally subject to monopolies*, the Czech Republic has started its policy of liberalising and opening up to competition certain sensitive sectors such as telecommunications and postal services.

The Ministry of Finance has been appointed as the monitoring authority for *state aid*. However, for the moment the system for the monitoring of state aid does not give the monitoring authority the possibility to assess the compatibility with the state aid rules of all aid measures granted by all public authorities or bodies appointed by the State to administer the aid. In particular, at present the monitoring authority does not monitor state aid granted by local authorities.

The latest aid inventory submitted in 1997 represents a significant step towards creating the transparency required in the granting of state aid to the industry. It shows that most of the objectives pursued are in line with those the EC rules. However, it includes solely aid financed by the state budget and does not give any information on aid granted by regional or local authorities.

Current and Prospective Assessment

The Czech Act on the Protection of Economic Competition represents a significant step towards greater harmonisation with EU *competition law* and the outstanding issues are currently being discussed between the Commission and the Office for the Protection of Competition.

The *Office for the Protection of Economic Competition* seems to have sufficiently qualified staff to enforce the law and the law is also applied in concrete cases.

Further information on measures which have been taken to liberalise telecommunication services need to be provided in order accurately to assess the situation in this sector. Progress is still also expected in the liberalisation of telecommunication infrastructures. Further information should also be provided on procedures for the licensing of services and infrastructures.

The Czech Republic has made significant progress in creating the transparency necessary for an efficient *state aid* control. The 1997 aid inventory for state aid granted in 1995 applies a methodology sufficiently close to that of the Community and contains almost all relevant information to get a good overview. However, the future inventory should cover all measures granted by the State, regional or local authorities or through public resources.

It is not yet entirely clear whether the monitoring authority on state aid has sufficient resources and powers to control the compatibility of all aid granted by all public authorities or bodies appointed by the State to administer the aid. Further clarifications are needed.

In addition to the adoption of legislation sufficiently approximate to that of the EC, *credible enforcement* of competition law requires the establishment of well functioning anti-trust and state aid monitoring authorities. It requires moreover that the judicial system, the public administration and the relevant economic operators have a sufficient understanding of competition law and policy.

Conclusion

Considerable progress has been made in terms of approximation of legislation in the field of *anti-trust*. The Office for the Protection of the Economic Competition seems to be sufficiently skilled to ensure the enforcement of the law and the efforts made so far by the Office represent an important step forward for a credible competition law enforcement.

In the field of *state aid* significant progress has been made as regards transparency in the granting of state aid. It is to be welcomed, moreover, that the Czech Government intends to limit the granting of state aid and to pursue a horizontal rather than a sectoral aid policy. However, the powers of the monitoring authority to examine the compatibility of all aid measures with the state aid rules need to be somewhat clarified and improved.

3.2. Innovation

Information Society

Present Situation

The economic and social effects made possible by the combination of information technology and telecommunications are great. In the Czech Republic these possibilities were neglected before 1989 although education generally was not. The result is that the size of the information technology (IT) market has recently spurted well beyond normal expectation deduced from GDP per capita. The existence of host computers on the Internet (4 per 1 000 inhabitants in January 1997), as a relative measure of development towards the information society (IS), suggests that the country has passed the position which the average EU country reached two years ago. The present telecommunications infrastructure may be operating as a brake on IS developments but the rapid rate of telecommunications modernisation should soon remove this problem.

Conclusion

Because of the positive approach to telecommunications liberalisation combined with the excellence of the national education system we can expect the Czech Republic to realise potentialities of the Information Society earlier than the average CEEC.

Education, Training and Youth

Articles 126 and 127 of the EC Treaty provide that the Community shall contribute to the development of quality education and implement a vocational training policy aimed at promoting the European dimension in education and at enhancing industrial adaptation and the responsiveness of the labour market through vocational training policies.

The Europe Agreement provides for co-operation in raising the level of education and professional qualifications.

The White Paper includes no measures in this field.

Descriptive Summary

The Czech Republic spending on education amounts to 5,9 % of GDP. It takes 14,6 % of the state budget.

There are 1 900 000 pupils, 190 000 students and 155 000 teachers in the Czech Republic.

There are 23 recognised universities, which depend on the Ministry of Education, and three Military Academies, which depend on the Ministry of Defence.

The Czech education system has reacted rapidly to the democratic changes in society and to the transformation of the economy. The changes in Czech education and training can be characterised by depolitisation, recognition of the right of pupils and adults to choose their own education and training, breaking down of the state monopoly; decentralisation in management and reform of the funding system.

The Federal Act of 1990 on Higher Education Institutions has given considerable independence and autonomy to faculties. However, university budgets are still exclusively covered by state budget. The Act does not allow for the development of non-state higher education.

Many changes were introduced in the vocational training policy since 1990. The general objectives for the forthcoming years include creation of a flexible system, creation of new skills (language, communication, information technologies), ongoing adaptation of curricula to labour market needs, and development of standards comparable to the Member States.

The Tempus programme has contributed to the achievement of the goals of higher education reform and created the basis for cooperation with the EU higher education institutions.

The Ministry of Education, Youth and Sports implements in co-operation with other ministries the programme for the Support and Protection of Children and Youth. This is the main instrument to support children and youngsters and their role in society.

Current and Prospective Assessment

Depolitisation of education and training has been achieved. The legal framework now needs to be strengthened and refined. Some of the priority areas for higher education are: diversification of financing of higher education institutions; improvement of university strategic management; diversification of higher education supply (private education, life-long learning, etc.); development of the non-university sector; integration of research and education; development of new curricula in key areas to increase awareness on EU issues (e.g. European studies), adaptation of curricula in EU regulated professions, accreditation and quality evaluation.

Although moving in the right direction, the vocational training system has developed towards democratisation and EU education standards in a rather deregulated way. A more strategic approach to be translated into legal reforms has still to be set up.

The Czech higher education and vocational training system is expected to meet EU standards in the medium term. The participation of Czech Republic in Community programmes will have positive effects and represent a good preparation for integration.

Conclusion

In the perspective of accession, no major problems should be expected in these fields.

Research and Technological Development

Research and Technological Development activities at Community level, as provided for by the Treaty and in the Framework Programme, aim at improving the competitiveness of European industry, the quality of life, as well as supporting sustainable development, environmental protection, and other common policies.

The Europe Agreement and its additional protocol provides for co-operation in these areas, notably through participation in the Framework Programme.

The White Paper includes no direct measures in this field.

Descriptive Summary

The Research and Development Council was established in 1992 under the Law on 'State Support of Scientific Activities and Technology Development' (amended in 1995), as a consultative body to the Government. Budget suggestions are passed through the Council from the different agencies to the Government and the Parliament. The law regulates the state funding of programmes in this sector, and defines the role of private research partners and of the state organs. The Grant Agency of the Czech Republic operates since 1993. It selects projects for grants on the basis of competitive peer evaluation. The Czech Academy of Sciences has undergone significant restructuring. Staff has been reduced from 14 000 to 5 000 and the number of institutions from over 100 to 59 plus 6 service institutions.

Expenditure for RTD represented 1,14% of GDP in 1995 and 1,21% in 1996 (*cf.* 2,12% in 1991). The share in the state budget expenditures for universities has risen considerably, from 26% in 1993 to 35% in 1996. This is now equivalent to what is spent for the Czech Academy of Sciences. An estimated 0,75% of GDP is spent on RTD by private enterprises. Research-industry relations are still fragile.

The general priorities of the government for this area are: intensification of research at universities, international co-operation, and improvement of the infrastructure. Priority subjects are: transfer of production technology to SMEs, protection of the environment, nuclear energy, transport infrastructure. Efforts are currently being made to improve infrastructure (7,5% of the total state budget allocated has to be spent on the support of infrastructure).

Regular cooperation with the European Union started in 1992 with the Thrid Research and Technology Development Framework Programme. So far, cooperation has mainly concentrated on Copernicus (Specific Programme for Cooperation with CECs and NIS) and remains rather low for participation in the Fourth Framework Programme. The Czech Republic is a member of COST (European cooperation in the field of scientific and technical research) and Eureka (European Research Coordination Agency).

Since 1995, the statistics in this field are compatible with OECD standards.

Current and Prospective Assessment

As one of the early industrialised countries in Europe, the Czech Republic has had a long-standing tradition of research and technological development, particularly in the field of engineering (machinery). It has invested much effort to restructure its scientific and technological institutions and expenditure. Now the Czech Republic will have to consolidate this sector to enable it to serve industrial innovation. The problem of the massive drop out from university (only 15% of the students enrolled achieve an academic qualification) will have to be addressed, as well as the upgrading of laboratory equipment.

An increased participation in Community programmes should help consolidate this sector and better serve the industrial innovation.

Conclusion

In the perspective of accession, no major problems are expected in this field. Accession would be of mutual benefit.

Telecommunications

The objectives of EC telecommunications policy are the elimination of obstacles to the effective operation of the Single Market in telecommunications equipment, services and networks, the opening of foreign markets to EU companies and the achievement of universally available modern services for EU residents and businesses. These are achieved through harmonisation of the standards and conditions for service offerings the liberalisation of the markets for terminals, services and networks and the adoption of necessary regulatory instruments. The Directives and policies needed to achieve this have now been established, but the liberalisation of public voice telephony and operation of related infrastructure will be deferred for a year or two after 1998 in certain Member States.

The Europe Agreement provides for co-operation aimed at enhancing standards and practices towards EC levels in telecommunication and postal policies, standardisation, regulatory approaches and the modernisation of infrastructure.

The White Paper focuses on the approximation of regulation, networks and services, followed by further steps ensuring gradual sector liberalisation.

Descriptive Summary

The penetration of telephone lines in the Czech Republic has expanded to over 25 per 100 by the end of 1995. The Czech Government's target is to reach a telephone lines penetration rate of 45 per 100 by the end of 2000.

After long internal debate, the Czech Government had adopted in a comprehensive policy for the telecommunications sector in August 1994. It consists of a) the partial privatisation of the existing (state-owned) Czech operating company (SPT) with a strategic partner and a voice monopoly until the year 2000, b) licensing of two mobile telephone networks using the pan-European digital standard (GSM) and c) the licensing of new local operators in sixteen localities. The privatisation was designed in such a way that the proceeds were used entirely to expand the capital stock of SPT. This enabled the company to reform its management structure and practices, and to implement a comprehensive investment programme. The second GSM licence was awarded so as to reinforce the competition resulting from the earlier reorganisation of the sector into separate cable and radio operators.

The Telecommunications Act of 1964 was amended in 1992 so as to separate clearly the regulatory role of the Government from the operational role of SPT. The regulatory authority is well staffed and functioning (the Czech Telecommunications Office) but the responsible minister exercises ownership rights over the principal operator.

The Postal Act of 1946, defines written communications and (temporarily) parcels and money orders as universal service obligations. New services, like international courier services, are now provided by international private operators in the Czech Republic.

Current and Prospective Assessment

Degree of Liberalisation

According to the commitments at the WTO negotiations in 1997, the Government will liberalise the market for the fixed network and voice telephony by 1 January 2000. The Government published its comprehensive, pro-competitive policy for the telecommunications sector in August 1994. It consists of a) the partial privatisation of the state-owned operating company (SPT) which holds a monopoly for long distance and international traffic, with a strategic partner, b) licensing of two mobile telephone networks using the pan-European digital standard (GSM) and c) the licensing of new local operators in sixteen localities. The first two items of this policy programme have been carried through successfully. The second GSM licence was awarded so as to reinforce the existing competition resulting from the long standing division of the sector into separate cable and radio operators.

Approximation to EC Law

The Telecommunications Act of 1964 was amended in 1992 (by the former Federal Government) so as to distinguish regulatory functions from operational ones. The changes also abolished the statutory monopolies, permitted privatisation, imposed licensing requirements on existing operators and thereby empowered the Government to adopt a policy of liberalisation. The policy of the Government is to complete their planned systematic transposition of EU Directives by the end of 2000. The regulatory authority is operational and administrative structures are sufficient to complete transposition of EC legislation.

A more effective separation of the regulatory and policy body from any operating company will be necessary to enable the Government to administer successfully a pro-competitive policy. Tariff rebalancing is well in hand although pricing policy is complicated by the division of powers between two Ministries. The difficulty of providing a service in the less advanced regions has been recognised by the Government and some measures have been taken. Stronger measures will be needed if universal service is to be achieved.

Infrastructure

The principal objective of Government policy has been to expand and modernise the public telecommunications networks and to improve the quality of services available. The privatisation of SPT was designed in such a way that the foreign capital was used entirely to increase the stock of the company. A reform of its management structures and practices has started. A comprehensive investment programme, including a new national digital 'backbone' network, is underway. Completion will help introduce advanced services especially in cities. Between 1991 and early 1997, the fixed network grew from 16,6 to 29,0 lines per 100 inhabitants compared to an average of 43,9 lines per 100 inhabitants for Greece, Portugal and Ireland. The Government target is to reach 45 lines per 100 inhabitants by the end of 2000. The Government decided early on that all new equipment added would be digital. The network is about 38% digitised as of January 1997 and the plan is to reach 60% by 2000 (compared to an average of 62,4% for Greece, Portugal and Ireland) and 100% by 2003. New GSM services commenced operations during 1996 and the number of cellular mobile users grew over 200% during the year to reach 183 000, i.e. 1,78 per 100 inhabitants. There is competition in both data services and satellite services. There were also 15,7 cable TV subscriptions and 7,4 PCs per 100 households in 1995.

Competitiveness of the Sector

At the beginning of 1997, there were 8,6 employees per 1 000 lines compared to an average of 6,2 for Greece, Portugal and Ireland. Even at today's high rate of network expansion, it will take a few more years before basic telephone services can be made universally available. Revenue per line (about 260 ECU in 1996), although among the highest in the region, will have to be sustained if the network is to be further expanded and the new operator to remain profitable. Provided that tariff rebalancing is continued, the telecommunications services sector should be able to face full liberalisation. SPT has already been able to obtain long term loans from EU commercial banks at interest rates lower than the EBRD's. The Dutch and Swiss operating companies paid 1,24 billion ECU jointly for 27% of SPT, the main Czech operator. The first mobile operator is 51% owned by SPT and 49% by a US consortium. The second operator is 51% owned by Ceske Radiokomunikace and 49% jointly by STET and a Germany company.

Conclusion

The Czech Republic should have little difficulty in complying with the *acquis* in the medium term provided that current efforts in transposition of laws and their implementation are continued. Tariffs must be further rebalanced in order to enable the public operator to take up competition.

Audio-visual

The audio-visual *acquis* aims, in the context of the internal market, for the provision and free movement of audio-visual services within the EU as well as the promotion of the European programme industry. The Television Without Frontiers Directive, which is applicable to all broadcasters regardless of the modes of transmission (terrestrial, satellite, cable) or their private or public nature, contains this *acquis*, setting down basic rules concerning transfrontier broadcasting. The main points are: to ensure the free movement of television broadcasts throughout Member States; to promote the production and distribution of European audio-visual works (by laying down a minimum proportion of broadcasting time for European works and those by independent producers); to set basic standards in the field of television advertising; to provide for the protection of minors and to allow for the right of reply.

The Europe Agreement provides for co-operation in the promotion and modernisation of the audio-visual industry, and the harmonisation of regulatory aspects of audio-visual policy.

The Television Without Frontiers Directives is a Stage I measure in the White Paper.

Descriptive Summary

The legal framework for the audio-visual sector is determined by Act No 468/1991, which provides for a dual system of broadcasting based on democratic principles.

The two main terrestrial television broadcasters are the national public service broadcaster Czech Television, and the commercial national broadcaster TV Nova.

The Czech film industry was privatised in the early 1990s and all direct state subsidies to the film production industry were cut. The film distribution sector is mainly made up of US programming.

Current and Prospective Assessment

The audio-visual sector in the Czech Republic is attempting to reestablish itself after major upheavals in recent years, and is characterised by rapid growth and constant change. Its ability properly to adhere to the *acquis* presupposes an upgrading of the capacity of the programme-making industry to meet the important challenges of an adapted regulatory framework.

Czech audio-visual legislation is not compatible with EC requirements; there are deficiencies remain in the areas of freedom of reception, the promotion of European and recent works, independent producers and isolated advertising spots.

In recent years the Czech Republic has made no progress in moving toward compliance with EC requirements in the audio-visual sector.

Conclusion

A major and concerted effort to adapt both the regulatory framework and industry structures will be needed if the Czech Republic is to meet EC requirements in the audio-visual sector in the medium term.

3.3. Economic and Fiscal Affairs

Economic and Monetary Union

By the time of the Czech Republic's accession, the third stage of EMU will have commenced. This will mark important changes for all Member States, including those that do not participate in the euro area. All Member States, including the new ones, will participate fully in the Economic and Monetary Union. Their economic policies will be a matter of common concern and they will be involved in the coordination of economic policies (national convergence programmes, broad economic guidelines, multilateral surveillance, excessive deficit procedure). They will be required to respect the stability and growth pact, to renounce any direct central bank financing of the public sector deficit and privileged access of public authorities to financial institutions, and to have completed the liberalisation of capital movements.

Accession means closer monetary and exchange rate co-operation with the European Union. This will require strengthening structural reforms in the area of monetary and exchange rate policies. Member States not participating in the euro area shall be able to conduct an autonomous monetary policy and participate in the European System of Central Banks (ESCB) on a restricted basis. Their central banks have to be independent and have price stability as their primary objective. Monetary policy has to be conducted with market-based instruments and has to be 'efficient' in transmitting its impulses to the real economy. Therefore, reforms need to be pursued to tackle factors that hinder the efficiency of monetary policy, such as the lack of competition in the banking sector, the lack of development of financial markets and the problem of 'bad loans' in the banking sector. Finally all Member States shall treat their exchange rate policy as a matter of common interest and be in a position to stabilise their exchange rates in a mechanism yet to be decided.

As membership of the European Union implies acceptance of the goal of EMU, the convergence criteria will have to fulfilled by the Czech Republic, although not necessarily on accession. While the fulfilment of the convergence criteria is not a precondition for EU membership, they remain key points of reference for stability oriented macroeconomics policies, and must in time be fulfilled by new Member States on a permanent basis. Hence the successful conclusion of systematic transformation and market oriented structural reforms is essential. The Czech Republic's economic situation and progress has already been analysed in preceding chapters of this Opinion.

Current and Prospective Assessment

The Central Bank is largely independent from the government in terms of the conduct of monetary policy and the appointment procedure of the Governor. The statutory objective of the Czech National Bank is to ensure the stability of the national currency, but this has been always interpreted in terms of price stability. The provisions concerning the possibility of the Central Bank to finance the budget deficit are still not in line with the Treaty requirements of explicit and complete prohibition. The Czech authorities are expected to reform the Law of the Central Bank to make it compatible with the Treaty requirements. In practice the Central Bank has never financed the budget deficit due to the sound fiscal record of the Czech Government to date.

Monetary policy in the Czech Republic has certainly been able to slow down inflation substantially. As the transition process gradually gained credibility from international markets, the tight monetary policy combined with a fixed exchange rate peg caused massive capital inflows in 1994/1995. These inflows were only partially sterilised and in 1995 money supply growth was well above the target, with inflation stuck at the previous year's level. The February 1996 widening of the bands around the central parity reduced the incentive for speculative capital inflows and since November 1996 inflation has resumed its downward path. The currency crisis of mid-May 1997 has led to a switch of the exchange rate regime from a currency peg to a managed float. There are still unresolved issues hindering the efficiency of monetary policy. The privatisation and the restructuring of the banking sector has to continue and bankruptcy procedures have to be enforced properly.

Between May 1993 and May 1997, the exchange rate was pegged to a basket consisting of USD and DM. Since May 1997, the Central Bank allows the exchange rate to float with an exchange rate target for the CZK-DM of 17-19,5 crown/mark. In the first phase of the transition, the exchange rate regime has proven to be successful in providing the system with a nominal anchor and bringing down inflationary expectations. When the progress of the transition led to a surge of speculative capital inflows (1994/1995), the authorities responded by widening the fluctuation band around the central parity (February 1996). The move helped to stop the capital inflows. However, the rising current account deficit, while not being an immediate threat for the stability of the exchange rate, has provoked a currency crisis of which the effects on the Czech economy are still unclear. In the new context, the fiscal authorities should take decisive action to sustain the disinflationary process by reducing public spending, and the pace of structural reforms should be increased.

Conclusion

It is premature to judge whether the Czech Republic will be in a position, by the time of its accession, to participate in the euro area; that will depend on the success of its structural transformation permitting to attain and to adhere permanently to the convergence criteria, which are not however a condition of accession.

The Czech Republic's participation in the third stage of EMU as a non-participant in the euro area should pose no problems in the medium term. Nonetheless Central Bank legislation should be made compatible with EC rules. Privatisation and competition in the banking sector has to be strengthened, as well as supervision in the financial markets.

Taxation

The *acquis* in the area of direct taxation mainly concerns some aspects of corporation taxes and capital duty. The four freedoms of the EC Treaty have a wider impact on national tax systems.

The indirect taxation *acquis* consists primarily of harmonised legislation in the field of Value Added Tax and excise duties. This includes the application of a non-cumulative general tax on consumption (VAT) which is levied on all stages of production and distribution of goods and services. This implies an equal tax treatment of domestic and non-domestic (import) transactions. The VAT *acquis* also contains transitional arrangements for the taxation of transactions within the European Union between taxable persons. In the field of excise duties the *acquis* contains harmonised tax structures and minimum rates of duty together with common rules on the holding and movement of harmonised excisable goods (including the use of fiscal warehouses). As a result of the introduction of the Single Market, all fiscal controls at the Community's internal frontiers were abolished in January 1993.

The mutual assistance between Member State tax authorities is an important feature of administrative cooperation in the internal market; the respective Directive covers both direct and indirect taxation.

The Europe Agreement contains provisions on approximation of legislation in the area of indirect taxation.

The White Paper contains as Stage I measures those which make up the main requirements of the indirect taxation *acquis* (essentially, those measures applied in the Community up to 1993),

and as Stage II measures those which are in addition necessary to implement the full indirect taxation *acquis*.

Descriptive Summary

Direct Taxation

The two company taxation Directives and the Arbitration Convention provide for a mechanism which applies on the basis of reciprocity. Respective provisions can therefore by definition not be expected to exist before accession.

Indirect Taxation

The overall contribution of VAT and excise duty revenue to the Czech Republic state budget was about 22% and 13% respectively in 1995. More recent statistics indicating trends in these figures are not currently available.

Value Added Tax

The current Czech VAT system was introduced on 1 January 1993 replacing the previous Single-Stage Turnover Tax. The Czech Republic applies a dual VAT rate system: a standard VAT rate of 22% and a reduced VAT rate of 5%. The standard rate applies in principle to all supplies of goods and certain specific services; whereas the reduced rate is applicable to most services and certain specific goods. With certain exceptions, imported goods are liable to VAT at the same rate as those supplied within the Czech Republic. In contrast, 'imported' services are not liable to any VAT.

Certain activities are exempt from VAT without the right to claim the input credit on such supplies. These exemptions relate mainly to activities in the public interest, financial and insurance services, property and lotteries and similar games. Taxable persons are in principle entitled to deduct VAT incurred on their purchases for business purposes of goods and services. The Czech Republic VAT Act does not at present contain any provisions enabling tax to be refunded to taxable persons not established within the country. However, as of 1 January 1998 such a refund scheme is planned to be introduced for supplies in relation to international transport, exhibitions and trade fairs.

Excise

The current system of excise duty in the Czech Republic was introduced at the same time as the VAT system. Excise duties are applicable to mineral oils, alcohol and alcoholic beverages and manufactured tobacco. For each product category, the duty is specific in nature.

Mutual Assistance

The tax administration has not yet had to develop its capacity for mutual assistance with the tax authorities of Member States, since mutual assistance is a feature which would only become applicable on accession.

Current and Prospective Assessment

Value Added Tax

The current VAT system in the Czech Republic has been based on the main principles of the VAT legislation of the Community. It is a solid starting point in its future alignments on the Community VAT *acquis*. However, it is characterised by being relatively brief and general in its application.

Foreign traders who are not permanently established in the Czech Republic and listed in the Commercial Register cannot be registered for VAT in the country. Since the Czech Republic does not operate any arrangements for the refund of VAT to non-registered foreign traders, VAT represents an increased cost to such traders. The application of the reduced VAT rate is notably broader in scope compared to the Community approach.

The Czech Republic's membership of the European Union would require adjustment to bring the VAT legislation into line with the requirements of the Community *acquis*. This is in particular the case as regards the system of taxation necessary in a Community with no internal frontier controls.

The Czech Republic national strategy plan for implementing the recommendations of the White Paper regarding VAT is planned to give priority to the elimination of the differences in the scope of VAT, including a narrowing of the scope of the application of the reduced VAT rate, a decrease of the registration threshold, provisions for VAT refunds to foreign taxable persons not established in the Czech Republic and a refund scheme for tourists. These changes are to be implemented gradually during 1998-2000.

Excise

There are significant discrepancies between the Czech excise regime and EU requirements.

Firstly, there exists no excise suspension system where goods can move between authorised tax warehouses without payment of duty.

Secondly, differences between the rates of the excise duty levied in the Czech Republic on similar products could lead to some distortion of competition between these products.

In order to ensure a correct application of the Community excise legislation it is essential that the Czech Republic sets up a warehousing system based on the Community model as soon as possible, and adapts the structure and level of its excise rates in such a way that they comply with the Community principle of non-discrimination between national products and those originating in other Member States.

The Czech national strategy plan for implementing the provisions of the White Paper does not provide a clear and detailed timetable for future adjustments of the Czech excise legislation. A short term objective consists of a gradual approximation of Czech legislation and the duty rates is not planned for the next 3-5 years.

Mutual Assistance

There would also be a need, on accession, to implement the appropriate arrangements for administrative cooperation and mutual assistance between Member States. These requirements are essential for the functioning of the internal market.

Conclusion

The *acquis* in respect of direct taxation should present no significant difficulties.

As regards indirect taxation, provided a sustained effort is made, the Czech Republic should be able to comply with the *acquis* concerning VAT and excise duties in the medium term.

It should be possible to start participating in mutual assistance as the tax administration develops its expertise in this respect.

Statistics

The main principles of the Community *acquis* relate to the impartiality, reliability, transparency, confidentiality (of individual information) and dissemination of official statistics. In addition there exists an important body of principles and practices concerning the use of European and international classifications, systems of national accounts, business registers, and various categories of statistics.

The Europe Agreement provides for co-operation to develop effective and reliable statistics, in harmony with international standards and classifications.

The White Paper includes no provisions in this field.

Descriptive Summary

The Czech Statistical Office (CSO) is the central body charged with co-ordinating official statistics in the Czech Republic.

The legal basis for Czech official statistics consists of the 1995 State Statistical Service Act.

Current and Prospective Assessment

Czech legislation is, with a few exceptions, compatible with the current standards applied within the European Union.

Some issues of transparency and confidentiality need attention, and there are deficiencies in sectors such as the business register, and regional, financial and agricultural statistics.

Conclusion

Provided that continuing progress is made, the Czech Republic should be able to comply with EU requirements for official statistics within the next few years.

3.4. Sectoral Policies

Industry

EC industrial policy seeks to enhance competitiveness, thus achieving rising living standards and high rates of employment. It aims at speeding up adjustment to structural change, encouraging an environment favourable to initiative, to the development of undertakings throughout the Community, and to industrial co-operation, and fostering better exploitation of the industrial potential of policies of innovation, research and technological development. EU industrial policy is horizontal by nature. Sectoral communications aim at transposing horizontal concepts into specific sectors. EU industrial policy results from an articulation of instruments from a number of Community policies; it includes both instruments related to the operation of markets (product specification and market access, trade policy, state aids and competitions policy) and measures related to industry's capacity to adapt to change (stable macroeconomic environment, technology, training, etc.).

In order to cope with competitive pressure and market forces within the Union, the industry of applicant countries needs to have achieved a certain level of competitiveness by the time of accession. The applicant countries need to be seen as pursuing policies aimed at open and competitive markets along the lines set out in Article 130 ('Industry') of the Treaty. Co-operation between the EC and the candidate countries in the fields of industrial co-operation, investment, industrial standardisation and conformity assessment as provided for in the Europe Agreement is also an important indicator of development in the right direction.

Descriptive Summary

The Czech Republic has a long industrial tradition. Its industrial structure was one of the most sophisticated in pre-war Europe. Before the transition prior to 1990 the country had become one of the most centrally-planned economies. The structure of the economy was dominated by industry (in particular mechanical engineering) and showed exceptional rigidity.

The transition since 1990 was accompanied by a sharp drop in industrial production. By 1995 the share of industrial production in GDP had dropped from a remarkably high 58% to 41% and stood at about 15 billion ECU, comparable to the industrial production of Greece. Total industrial employment has been declining and now stands at about 2 million. Small firms account for more than 98% of all industrial firms, but only for 2,5% of industrial employment while the rest, medium-sized and large firms, provide the lion's share in employment.

Machinery and *equipment* industry has a long tradition in production of standard medium and low-range machines. It is highly specialised and an important manufacturing sector within industry, with close links to German and Austrian producers. Despite low productivity the industry is able to export over half of production, especially to the EU (mainly Germany), largely because of low labour costs.

Agri-food industries: except for some large firms the sector has been completely privatised and attracted FDI coming mainly from the EU. The *steel sector* essentially consists of three large firms. Despite positive first steps privatisation halted and a large part of the shares are still in state ownership. Since the Government decided not to take further restructuring steps before full privatisation, the necessary fundamental restructuring is overdue. The industry is considerably oversized in relation to internal consumption and the demand for public aid or for capacity closure may rise.

Czech Industry, Main Production Sectors in 1995

Sector	%-share industrial production (value added)	%-share industrial employment
Raw material processing (including mettalurgy, cement, glass, ceramics, paper and wood)	21	22
Metal, mechanical and electrical products	15	20
Agri-food	12	8
Construction	12	16
Chemicals	12	5
Automotive industry	6	6,5
Information technology	4,5	2
Textiles, clothing and leather	3,5	10
Pressure equipment, medical and meteorological equipment	2,5	2,5
Pharmaceuticals	2	0,5
Total of the above	90,5	92,5
Other industries	9,5	7,5
Total Industry	100	100
Industrial production (excluding construction) as % GDP	*34*	

The *non-ferrous metals sector* is much smaller and most domestic demand is met by imports. The *chemical sector* is a relatively large sector. Restructuring is in full progress: 80% of production now originates from the private sector.

The *automotive industry* is second only to the Polish industry in terms of production in the CEECs. The passenger car market is dominated by one single car maker, majority-owned by a German manufacturer. Through FDI product quality has improved and EU suppliers are shifting production to take advantage of low production and labour costs. Car production in 1995 reached 200 000 of which nearly half was exported, mainly to the EU. Production is expected to double after 1997, directed partly to EU markets.

The *metal products industry* is specialised in high value products and has a skilled workforce. To attain economies of scale most firms need exports to survive and, despite low productivity levels, low labour costs permit the industry to export more than half of its low-price production to the EU. Imports are also mainly from the EU, underlining close links of the industry with EU industry.

The *textiles, clothing* and *leather sectors* were hard hit by the reform shocks and production fell steeply. Privatisation of large firms in the textiles and clothing sectors has been completed and foreign investment is directed toward modernisation. Relatively low labour costs allow trade with the Union with around half of textiles and clothing trade and production directly linked to further processing for EU firms (outward processing trade or OPT). However, further structural adjustments will become inevitable once labour costs rise.

The *mining industry* is a net exporter and is considered competitive. Privatisation is nearly completed and has attracted significant participation of a number of EU firms, notably in the cement sector.

The *pharmaceutical industry* is small but relatively strong and modern and did not experience decline during transformation despite pressures from sector liberalisation and imports. Privatisation is progressing well and the industry has succeeded in attracting foreign capital. The many licensing agreements with Western manufacturers and successful R & D programmes show high standards and technical competence. However, relatively low investment levels in basic R & D seem unlikely to yield significant results levels. The industry thus relies on the production of (branded) generics.

The *paper* and *wood sector* is of modest size and relies on small but well located forest resources. The graphical and printing industry is a driving force due to foreign demand, and the sector has attracted foreign investment.

Multinational companies have established a presence in the small *information technology sector*, concentrating on a small range of products and electronic parts. The Czech Republic is considered one of the most dynamic IT markets among the CEECs. Production growth is lagging far behind domestic demand expansion but considerable production growth is expected.

It appears that most of Czech industry, based on a well trained labour force and an advantageous location in the centre of Europe has comparative advantages, with lacking productivity levels being compensated by low wage levels thus assuring their current price competitiveness. Foreign direct investment has aided restructuring efforts, which have varied according to sectors. Typically competitiveness appears assured as long as current low cost conditions for wages and other production costs in sectors of high labour intensity in a wide low to medium range of industrial technology: machinery and equipment, non ferrous metals, fabricated metal products, building materials, mineral mining, chemicals, pharmaceuticals, passenger cars, railway equipment, textile and clothing, pressure equipment, paper, wood and printing. High tech industries, such as information technologies and medical equipment are clearly import dominated and heavy industries, like steel, remain state owned, mostly unrestructured and in manifest crisis with excess capacities overdue for restructuring.

Current and Prospective Assessment

According to most indicators the Czech Republic is no longer in transition.

There are a number of positive factors for Czech industry. There are few barriers to trade. Exports account for a large share of the economy (over 50%) and industrial output. Further, the share of investment in GDP (30%) is as large as that of some of the ASEAN tigers. The infrastructure should thus improve rapidly. The *acquis* is being adopted at a satisfactory pace, and the prospects for effective implementation are relatively good. Provided that rising wage and other production costs do not erode these advantages within this promising environment, Czech industry should be able to grow quickly and gain in competitiveness. Within the next five years it may reach a level that is comparable to that of Portugal.

The main problems lie in the area of corporate governance. Banks face conflicts of interests as the owners of the investment funds that own large parts of industry and as creditors to the same enterprises they often also dominate. This combination has reduced restructuring and might explain the current low level of unemployment and bankruptcies. Moreover, given the weak balance sheets of many banks they are not likely to provide the financing required for adjustment. All this weakens the capacity of Czech industry to change and adapt to its two main challenges: adoption of the *acquis* and competition from low wage producers as Czech wages increase.

Another handicap for industry is the dominant role of large enterprises and their heavy consumption of energy. Over the next decade many of the large energy intensive enterprises in heavy industry will have to undergo radical adjustment.

Conclusion on Industrial Competitiveness

Provided that past and current efforts at restructuring and modernisation are continued — and reinforced in case of heavy industries — most sectors of Czech industry should face no major problems to integrate into the enlarged EU market in the medium term. Yet in the long run, efforts towards enhanced non-price competitiveness and productivity of Czech industry need to be undertaken to maintain competitiveness in view of likely increased wage and production costs.

An evaluation of the *acquis* specific to the free circulation of industrial goods is to be found in the separate section on the internal market

Agriculture

The Common Agricultural Policy aims to maintain and develop a modern agricultural system ensuring a fair standard of living for the agricultural community and the supply of food at a reasonable price for consumers, and ensuring the free movement of goods within the EC. Special attention is given to the environment and rural development. Common market organisations exist to administer the CAP. These are complemented by regulations on veterinary health, plant health and animal nutrition and by regulations concerning food hygiene. Legislation also exists in the area of structural policy, originally developed primarily to modernise and enlarge agriculture, but more recently with an increasing emphasis on the environment, and the regional differentiation of the policy. Since reforms in 1992, increasing contributions to farm support have come from direct aid payments increasingly compensating for reduced market support prices.

The Europe Agreement provides the basis for agricultural trade between Czech Republic and the Community and aims to promote co-operation on the modernisation, restructuring and privatisation of Czech Republic's agriculture sector as well as the agro-industrial sector and phyto-sanitary standards.

The White Paper covers the fields of veterinary, plant health and animal nutrition controls, as well as marketing requirements for individual commodities. The purpose of such legislation is to protect consumers, public health and the health of animals and plants.

Descriptive Summary

Agricultural Situation

The value of the agricultural production in 1995 was approximately 1,79% of that of the Union.

In 1995, agriculture accounted for 6,3% of employment and 5,2% of the GDP. Of the total area of 7,9 million hectares, 4,3 million hectares is used for agricultural purposes, with arable land taking up 3,1 million hectares, whilst forests cover 2,6 million hectares. Half of the arable land is under cereals (about 1,6 million hectares in 1995), mainly wheat and barley. However, in recent years there has been a shift to cereals, while oilseeds have doubled their share over the period.

Total agricultural output has diminished by about 28% since 1989. The livestock sector has been the most affected over the transition period, with output dropping by over 30% (cattle -40%; sheep -50%). Crop output has decreased by about 20%.

In 1995, however, agriculture recorded a turnaround. Gross output was up by 4,2%, following a continuous fall in output since 1989. Production in 1995 reached around 85% of its 1989 level. As to land ownership, the main objectives of the reform policy of 1991-1994 were to re-establish private property rights in agriculture through restitution of land, transformation of the agricultural co-operatives and the land law. 98,8% of the claims were settled by the end of 1995.

Individual private farms manage about one third of the agricultural land. In 1994 most individual private farms (40 000 out of 50 000) were of less than 10 hectares, mainly producing for own consumption or local markets. The remaining individual farms (10 000) could be considered as professional farms, with the largest (over 100 hectares) farming on mainly leased land and with equipment rented from the State on the basis of annual contracts. The transformed co-operatives (over 1 300) were still managing half of the agricultural land with an average size of 1 600 hectares. Several reasons contributed to the fact that many of the old collective farms have continued as co-operatives (fragmentation of ownership into small plots of land, the general atmosphere of uncertainty in the transitional years and lack of entrepreneurial skills and financial resources). Other agricultural enterprises (nearly 1 300 in number with an average size of 600 hectares) were managing over 15% of the agricultural land.

In 1995, the Czech Republic produced 6,6 million tonnes cereals, 1,3 million tonnes potatoes, 662 000 tonnes oilseeds, 550 000 tonnes vegetables; in 1994 it produced 3,2 million tonnes milk, 184 000 tonnes beefmeat, 465 000 tonnes porkmeet and 121 000 tonnes poultry meat.

Ownership changes have taken place in the agrofood industry, but restructuring to deal with overcapacities is still underway.

The Czech Republic is a net importer of food and agricultural products; in 1995 exports reached 1 213 millions ECU (264 million ECU to EU) and imports 1 690 million ECU (753 million ECU from EU). The main export market for agricultural products (1996) is the EU (36,4%) and the Slovak Republic (27,3%). 14,9% of exports went to the New Independent States, 0,8% to EPTA and 9,7% to other CEECs. Main exported products are dairy products, beverages, beer, livestock, hops, malt, and meat and meat products.

Agri-food imports mainly come from the EU (54,3% of total agri-food imports in 1996) and the Slovak Republic (8,9%). 1,3% of imports came from EFTA, 6,9% from other CEECs and 0,3% from the NIS. Imports include fruits, coffee, tea, cocoa, vegetables, soya cakes, and grain.

Agricultural Policy

The PSE (producer subsidy equivalent) calculated by the OECD was 14% in 1995, compared to 49% for the EU.

The Czech Republic's agricultural policy has four main principles: a) price stability; b) food security; c) environmental quality; and d) foreign market access. In 1996, total expenditure on agriculture increased by 12% compared to the previous budget (net expenditure of the State on agricultural support amounted to 8,9 billion CZK in 1995).

Agricultural policy in the Czech Republic is relatively liberal and market regulations exist for only a few essential products (wheat, dairy products). Measures include intervention buying and in particular export subsidies.

Price levels are generally significantly lower than EC prices. The current price gap at producer level for the main crop products lies at 15 to 20% and is somewhat smaller than the price gap for the main livestock products, milk and beef, which can be assessed at around 30% (partially due to quality differences). For the cereals-based meats, pork and poultry, the price gap is non-existent or much smaller than could be expected on the basis of the cereals price differential.

Rural development and environmental policies are receiving increasing attention and funding of rural and structural development programmes aimed at supporting farmers in less favoured areas, creating off-farm employment and promoting environmentally friendly farming, has been increased substantially in recent years.

The Czech Republic has undertaken commitments in the GATT Agreement on domestic support, market access and export subsidies. The commitments are made in national currency. Minimum access quotas were opened for 27 groups of products in 1995 such as beef, pork, poultry and dairy products. Export support, which is in particular concentrated on meat and dairy products, is limited to 4,34 billion CZK (105 million ECU) in the year 2000.

The trade arrangements under the Europe Agreement, providing in agriculture for mutual import tariff preferences, have been in force since 1994.

The Czech Republic has also concluded several bilateral or regional agreements with an aim to develop trade: the Czech-Slovak Customs Union from 1 January 1993; the Central European Free Trade Area (CEFTA) with the Slovak Republic, Poland, Hungary and Slovenia, which foresees progressive liberalisation of agricultural trade. Free trade agreements with EFTA countries, Romania, Bulgaria, Estonia, Latvia, and from 1 January 1997 with Lithuania and Israel were also concluded. Negotiations are under way with Turkey and a Free Trade Agreement will be negotiated with Croatia, Morocco, Tunisia, Malta and Cyprus.

The Czech Republic is in the process of harmonising its legislation following the recomendations of the White Paper.

The Czech Republic has an institutional infrastructure with a certain number of agencies managing different aspects of Czech agricultural policy under the central responsiblity of the Ministry of Agriculture.

Most agricultural organisations and associations in the food production processing and distribution industries are associated in a National Chamber of Agriculture, which was established in 1993 on a legal basis and with government financial support.

Current and Prospective Assessment

Given the relatively limited importance of agriculture in the overall economy, the agricultural sector is not a main priority in the government's policies.

In the longer run (5-10 years) agricultural production is expected to increase to reach level prior to transition and exceed consumption in key areas like cereals, oilseed, dairy and meat products. The most significant problems still seem to concern low yields, quality of the products, low level of profitability, an inefficient agro-food industry still in the process of restructuring that is hampered by severe financial difficulties and overcapacity, insufficient environmental protection and lack of adequate market information in certain parts of the marketing chain.

In general, the main market policy instruments applied in the EG are not applied in the Czech Republic. This includes key instruments like quotas (dairy, sugar sectors) and the arable crop scheme (base area, set-aside compensatory payment schemes), premia in the livestock sector (cattle identification and registration systems), producer organisations in the fruit and vegetable sectors, as well as certain rural and structural development programmes.

Management and control of these measures would require relatively sophisticated administrative systems, including an appropriate land register and cattle identification and registration systems. As a general observation, it is clear that the administrative capacity would need to be further development in these areas if these measures were to be applied in the Czech Republic. Market price quotation systems would also be required for market management purposes.

It is difficult to foresee at this stage what will be the development of agricultural support prices in the Czech Republic in the period before accession; this will depend on a number of factors including the domestic economy, the situation on export markets, and the development of price support levels in the Union.

Although progress has been made in adapting rural and structural policies, a number of measures appears to be inconsistent with EC policies.

Negotiations are on going to solve the difficulties which have arisen in the application of the trade provisions of the Europe Agreement.

The Czech Republic is making progress in introducing the legislation identified in the White Paper.

However, differences with the *acquis* still remain in the veterinary and phytosanitary field. An agreement on equivalency in the veterinary and phytosanitary field is being finalised with the Czech Republic. The annexes to the agreement identify the items on which equivalency can be agreed and on which further negotiations are necessary.

In the veterinary field progress on approximation to, and implementation of the *acquis* is depending on the progress on the adoption and implementation of the new veterinary Act, which is envisaged to enter into force by December 1997. Preparation of secondary legislation is initiated.

The Czech Republic has a well established infrastructure for veterinary control and inspection, both at the borders and internally. The facilities at border inspection posts and testing laboratories appear to be adequate to carry out appropriate control and testing according to internal market requirements. Procedures, frequencies and results of veterinary checks at the external borders are similar to those applied in EC Member States. There is, however, a need to upgrade testing and inspection facilities.

Although the legislation under preparation appears to a large extent to be consistent with the *acquis*, further adaptation would be needed in particular with regard to identification and registration of animals, the licensing system, introduction of HACCP (Hazard Analysis Critical Control Panel) and self-control systems and veterinary checks. Furthermore, it appears that some of the basic principles of the internal market, such as the concept of safeguard measures and import rules, have not been reflected entirely in the current primary legislation.

There will be a need to upgrade certain food processing establishments in particular for the national market, to develop acceptable veterinary audit and certification procedures, and to maintain an adequately structured, resourced, staffed and trained veterinary sector.

The full implementation of the *acquis* should be achievable during the preaccession period if adequate funds are made available from the state budget.

With reference to the phytosanitary field the situation is the following: as regards seeds and propagation material it is stated that the legislation and necessary administrative arrangements are compatible with EC legislation. No major problems are foreseen particularly as the country is already a member of OECD and enjoys Community equivalence under the seed legislation for the majority of EU species. The framework legislation on plant health for approximation to EC legislation came into force on 1 January 1997. As regards regulation on plant protection products, harmonisation of legislation with Community legislation is envisaged to begin in 1997. As regards legislation on animal nutrition, pesticide residues and organic farming, it is difficult at this stage to establish the level of approximation to Community rules. The Czech Republic will need to ensure that this EC legislation is implemented in national legislation.

Conclusion

Further alignment to the *acquis* is still necessary, although significant progress has been made in adopting the measures mentioned in the White Paper.

Particular efforts are needed in relation to:

☐ implementation and enforcement of veterinary and phytosanitary requirements and upgrading of establishments to meet EC standards;

☐ strengthening of the administrative structures to ensure the necessary capacity to implement and enforce the policy instruments of the CAP;

☐ further restructuring of the agri-food sector to improve its competitive capacity.

If such progress is accomplished, accession in the medium term should not be accompanied by significant problems in applying the common agricultural policy in an appropriate manner.

Fisheries

The Common Fisheries Policy includes common market organisations, structural policy, agreements with third countries, management and conservation of fish resources, and scientific research in support of these activities.

The Europe Agreement includes provisions concerning trade in fisheries products with the Community.

The White Paper includes no measures in this field.

Descriptive Summary

The Czech Republic has only inland water fisheries. In 1994 catch was 22 600 tonnes — mainly carp. No information was provided on processing fish.

As a trading partner of the Community, the Czech Republic represents 0,17% of EU total imports (independently of origin) of fisheries products and 6,8% of EU imports of fisheries products from the candidate countries alone (in terms of value). As regards EU exports, the Czech Republic receives 1,31% of our total exports of fisheries products and 15,8% of our exports of these products to the candidate countries (in terms of value).

Current and Prospective Assessment

Czech Republic's production and foreign trade data, when compared to the corresponding EU figures, are quite low and therefore they should not have a significant impact upon the Community as a whole.

It will be necessary for the Czech Republic to ensure compliance with the EU's health, hygiene and environmental standards.

Conclusion

This sector should not represent a problem for accession

Energy

The main EU energy policy objectives, as reflected in the Commission White Paper 'An energy policy for the EU' include enhancement of competitiveness, security of energy supplies and protection of the environment. Key elements of the energy *acquis* comprise of Treaty provisions and secondary legislation particularly concerning competition and state aids, internal energy market (including directives on electricity price transparency, gas and electricity transit, hydrocarbons, licensing, emergency response including security stock obligations, etc.), nuclear energy, as well as energy efficiency and environmental rules. Development of Trans-European Energy Networks and support for energy R & D are other important elements of energy policy. Ongoing developments include liberalisation of the gas sector, energy efficiency *acquis* and the Auto-oil programme.

In the field of nuclear energy, the Community *acquis* has evolved substantially from the original EAEC Treaty to a framework of legal and political instruments, including international agreements. At present, it addresses issues of health and safety, including radiation protection, safety of nuclear installations, management of radioactive waste, investment including Euratom financial instruments, promotion of research, nuclear common market, supplies, safeguards, and international relations.

The Europe Agreement provides for co-operation to develop the progressive integration of the energy markets in Europe and includes provisions on assistance within the related policy areas.

The White Paper preparing CEECs for the internal energy market, underlines the need for full application of key internal market directives in combination with EC competition law. As to the nuclear sector, the White Paper refers to nuclear supply safeguards and shipments of nuclear waste.

Descriptive Summary

The Czech energy situation is dominated and will be dominated by domestic solid fuels (hard coal and lignite), representing 60% of the energy balance and causing serious environmental damage, particularly in the Northern Region (e.g. Black Triangle). For its oil and gas supplies (17,5% respectively 14% of energy needs), the country is dependent on external sources, particularly on Russia. Uranium mining (600 tU/year) will continue until 2001.

Mine closures resulted in a decrease of hard coal production from 22 million tonnes in 1990 to 16 million tonnes in 1995. Lignite production decreased from 90 to 56 million tonnes over the period 1989-1995. From 1989-1994 the labour force was reduced by more than 50% reaching a level of 82 000.

The Czech Republic is, with a view to diversification, increasingly inter-connected with the European Union. The synchronous test connection since 1995 to the Western European UCPTE electricity network as well as the link up of the Czech refineries with Germany should be noted.

The energy sector is two to three times less efficient than the EU-average due to, for example, the past supply oriented policies and low prices.

The Czech Republic has four Russian designed VVER 213 nuclear reactors at Dukovany (modernisation programme ongoing) the safety of which is considered to be close to safety objectives generally accepted in the EU once upgrading programmes are implemented. There are two VVER 1000 under construction at Temelin (with integration of US technology). Around the year 2000 the share of nuclear in electricity production may increase from 22 to 40%. Three research reactors are also in operation, using fuel fabricated in Russia.

Current and Prospective Assessment

The Czech energy policy is in line with EC objectives such as: ensuring security of energy supplies including diversification; introducing market principles; and protecting the environment and increasing energy efficiency.

The competition framework in the energy sector is progressively approximating with the directives of the internal energy market in combination with the application of EU competition law. The basic competition legislation is applicable to the energy sector and the 1994 Energy Act defines the State's role in the energy subsectors and provides a framework for sector regulation.

Privatisation is underway in various subsectors but the State retains monopolies or dominant positions in electricity production and trade, uranium production, oil and gas pipeline transport. Independent power producers and industrial self-producers increase gradually their share in the electricity production.

Despite considerable increases, gas, electricity and heat prices for households are cross-subsidised by industry and do not recover cost. The Government is expected to decide in the summer 1997 on a policy to reach cost levels by the year 2000.

Current emergency oil stocks are estimated at forty days of consumption, well below the EU target of ninety. In the event of a rapid adoption of the necessary legislation (summer 1997) full compliance with EC *acquis* is expected within six to eight years.

Restructuring of the mining sector (solid fuels and uranium) will continue beyond the year 2000. Its social and regional consequences will have to be addressed, whereas State interventions should be assessed against EC and ECSC State aid rules.

The Czech Republic has started the development of Community conform efficiency legislation (e.g. labelling appliances, minimum efficiency norms) as well as environmental norms (e.g. fuel quality standards), but more remains to be done. Adoption of an Energy Saving Law (expected summer 1997) will underpin future compliance with the efficiency *acquis*. It should be noted that the upgrading of refineries to meet EC standards will require considerable investments and these refineries will have to compete on a saturated European market.

Concerning uranium mining, the obligation for the national electricity company to buy in the event of nuclear fuels import, an equivalent amount of domestic uranium in principle infringes upon the rules of the nuclear common market but will be phased out by 2000. Uranium supply (if not from domestic source), enrichment services and fuel fabrication services are covered by contracts with various firms in several countries. The common nuclear materials supply policy of security through diversification of sources would apply on accession for supply contracts concluded after accession. It would be desirable for the Czech Republic to continue with its plans to diversify its supply sources.

Spent nuclear fuel is presently stored on site. A longer term interim repository is projected to start around 2005 for both Dukovany and Temelin fuels. A decision on whether to reprocess spent fuel or dispose of it as waste is not expected before 2015.

Upon accession, the Czech Republic would need to comply with the provisions of the Euratom Treaty, in particular those related to supply of nuclear material, the nuclear common market, safeguards, health and safety and international agreements. As it is already party to all international nuclear regimes and has a full-scope safeguards agreement in force with the IAEA, no major difficulties in applying Community legislation are expected in this and the other areas mentioned above. Special attention has to be given to timely implementation of nuclear safety programmes. The development of a nuclear safety authority should be supported.

Conclusion

Provided that current efforts are maintained, the Czech Republic should be in a position to comply with most of the EC energy legislation in the next few years. However, matters such as the adjustment of monopolies including import and export issues, access to networks, energy pricing, emergency preparedness including the building up of mandatory oil stocks, state interventions in the solid fuels and uranium sectors, and the development of energy efficiency and fuel quality standards need to be closely followed.

No major difficulties are foreseen for compliance with Euratom provisions. The nuclear safety standards should be tackled appropriately in order to bring all the nuclear plants to the safety level required; and longer term solutions for waste have to be defined.

Transport

Community transport policy consists of policies and initiatives in three fundamental areas:

☐ improving quality by developing integrated and competitive transport systems based on advanced technologies which also contribute to environmental and safety objectives;

☐ improving the functioning of the Single Market in order to promote efficiency, choice and user-friendly provision of transport services while safeguarding social standards;

☐ broadening the external dimension by improving transport links with third countries and fostering the access of EU operators to other transport markets (The Common Transport Policy Action programme, 1995-2000).

The Europe Agreement provides for approximation of legislation with Community law and cooperation aimed at restructuring and modernising transport, improving access to the transport market, facilitating transit and achieving operating standards comparable to those in the Community.

The White Paper focuses on measures for accomplishing internal market conditions in the transport sector, including such aspects as competition, legislative harmonisation and standards.

Descriptive Summary

The geographical situation of the Czech Republic, bordering on the present frontiers of the European Union and marking an intersection of North-South and East-West communication routes, makes it a transit country between the Member States and the applicant countries. It is traversed by two pan-European transport corridors. The political changes at the beginning of the 1990s led to a significant increase in traffic flows, including transit traffic. Although the road network is, on the whole, relatively well developed, it is still unable to cope with road transport demand, which almost doubled between 1990 and 1995. The modal distribution has altered distinctly to the detriment of rail and inland waterway transport and there has been a marked decrease in collective passenger road transport due to a rapid rise in the ownership and use of private vehicles. Air transport is expanding at a steady rate (20% per year at Prague Airport).

Current and Prospective Assessment

As regards completion of the internal market, the Czech Republic has made relatively good progress in adoption of the *acquis*. The Czech international transport sector already broadly applies rules similar to those of the Community, in particular in the air, maritime, inland waterway, combined transport and passenger road transport fields. In the case of rail transport, care should be taken to ensure the effective application of the *acquis;* the public service aspects and standardisation of accounts need to be monitored over the next few years. The road haulage sector complies with most of the provisions of the *acquis* with regard to international traffic but the operation of its domestic arm poses greater potential risks. This aspect will require close attention and is of particular importance in the context of a future Union without internal frontiers, when road haulage cabotage will be totally unrestricted. The Czech Republic will also have to align itself with the Community in respect of roadworthiness tests and road taxation.

The development of an integrated and competitive transport system is an objective of which the Czech authorities are aware; achieving an acceptable level of safety and optimal use of the transport system are likely to be the two main difficulties. The Czech Republic's progress on safety is satisfactory. In contrast, the objective of coherence in the transport system appears harder to attain. The Czech Republic is likely to face a steady rise in the share of road transport and will have to focus its efforts on the use of railways and inland waterways.

In order to improve links with the Member States and its neighbours, the Czech Republic is planning to invest about 2,7 billion ECU of its own budget over the period 1995-1999 in transport infrastructure used by international traffic, primarily trans-European corridors. This sum amounts to a respectable 1,2 % of GNP, yet even this will not necessarily cover needs. Any reduction in this amount as a result of budgetary constraints would only serve to exacerbate this relative shortcoming.

Conclusion

The Czech Republic has made notable progress in the adoption of the *acquis* in the transport sector. Provided that it improves the operation of its domestic road haulage market (in particular on market access, safety rules and tax) and the financial transparency of the rail sector, the transport sector is unlikely to pose major problems as regards adoption of the internal market *acquis*.

It will be necessary, however, to make sure that the resources needed to lay the foundations for the future trans-European transport network extended to include the new member countries, are made available. It would also be advisable for the Czech Republic's administrative structures, and in particular bodies supervising areas such as safety, to be rapidly reinforced.

Small and Medium Enterprises

EU enterprise policy aims at encouraging a favourable environment for the development of SMEs throughout the EU, at improving their competitiveness and encouraging their Europeanisation and internationalisation. It is characterised by a high degree of subsidiarity. The complementary role of the Community is defined and implemented through a Multiannual Programme for SMEs in the EU. This programme provides the legal and budgetary basis for the Community's specific SME policy actions. The *acquis* has so far been limited to recommendations on specific areas, although legislation in other sectors also affects SMEs (e.g. competition, environment, company law).

The Europe Agreement provides for co-operation to develop and strengthen SMEs, in particular in the private sector, *inter alia* through provision of information and assistance on legal, administrative and tax conditions.

The White Paper contains no specific measures.

Descriptive Summary

The current Czech definition of SME covers enterprises with up to 500 employees.

The vast majority of enterprises are SME and 87 % of them are very small. In industry, all of 98,5 % of companies have less than 50 employees. The main sectors in terms of number of enterprises are retail or wholesale trade (ca 30 %) and services (ca. 30 %), followed by the manufacturing industry (ca. 15 %) and construction (ca. 15 %).

Important modifications in the employment structure have taken place, in particular the absorption of part of the redundant labour force from agriculture and large state firms by small and medium sized enterprises, especially in the service sector.

Current and Prospective Assessment

Since 1991, the support for the small and medium enterprises (SME) as part of the private sector development has been an important key to economic and employment growth in the Czech Republic.

All general regulations for establishing and operating business apply also to SMEs in their entirety, so no distinction is made according to size. An extensive network of regional advisory and information centres has now been set up to support the development of small and medium size enterprises, covering most of the territory of the Czech Republic. Two SME funding operations for loans and guarantees have been launched.

The basic legal and support structures are in place, but there is a need for further refinement and increased coherence in policy for SMEs.

The on-going efforts to strengthen the SMEs during the pre-accession period will therefore need to be continued.

Conclusion

There are no specific problems regarding the Czech Republic's participation in this field.

3.5. Economic and Social Cohesion

Employment and Social Affairs

Community social policy has been developed through a variety of instruments such as legal provisions, the European Social Fund and actions focused on specific issues, including public health, poverty and the disabled. The legal *acquis* covers health and safety at work, labour law and working conditions, equal opportunities for men and women, social security co-ordination for migrant workers and tobacco products. Social legislation in the Union has been characterised by laying down minimum standards. In addition, the social dialogue at European level is enshrined in the Treaty (Article 118B), and the Protocol on social policy refers to consultation of the social partners and measures to facilitate the social dialogue.

The Europe Agreement provides for approximation of legislation and co-operation on improving standards of health and safety at work, labour market policies and the modernisation of the social security system. It also provides for Community workers legally employed in the Czech Republic to be treated without discrimination on grounds of nationality as regards their working conditions.

The White Paper provides for measures for approximation in all the areas of the *acquis*.

Descriptive Summary

In the field of *social dialogue* there are a number of organisations for employees. The most representative is the Czech and Moravian Chamber of Trade Unions which is a member of the European Trade Union Confederation (ETUC). On the employers' side, the main association is the Confederation of Employers which has joined the Union of Industrial and Employers' Conference of Europe (UNICE). Generally, the Government's policies have not helped to encourage employers to negotiate within the framework of the social dialogue. The trade unions are concerned that the Government does not take account of the opinion of the social partners, except on questions linked to wages and working conditions of a company. The social dialogue is not yet well established.

Since 1993, the Czech Republic has enjoyed a low rate of *unemployment*. In 1996, according to ILO methodology, it was 3,4 %.. Unemployment is higher in mono-sector areas. It is disputed whether the statistics reflect the real employment situation. The tight labour market has been an extraordinary feature of the Czech transformation process until now. But the necessary economic restructuring is expected to lead to higher unemployment.

A network of regional and local employment offices has been established to implement *labour market policies*. The Czech Republic has successfully embarked upon a policy to make the labour market more flexible and to develop the appropriate mechanisms for functioning labour markets. With a continued effort to supplement this with an appropriate range of labour market policy measures, this should ensure an efficient allocation of labour and a capacity for continuous adaptation to structural change.

With the exception of employment policy (share of total contribution: 0,2 % of GDP), the pattern of spending is similar to the EU Member States: the largest share of total expenditure on *social security* is spent on pensions (8,8 % of GDP), followed by health care expenditure (8,1 % of GDP-1995 figures). The rapid growth in the health sector's share of GDP (the share has risen from 5,4 % in 1991 to 8,1 % in 1995) brings the Czech Republic close to the OECD average. This increase has been accompanied by improved welfare for the population. Continued efforts are required to ensure that measures of social protection are developed.

The Czech *health system* needs to be improved.

Current and Prospective Assessment

The Czech Republic has agreed a set of general principles concerning the protection of *health and safety at work*, but improvements will need to be made on the approximation of legislation for the protection of health and safety of workers in specific areas. The Czech Republic has independent inspection structures in accordance with the ILO Convention No 81. The means at the disposal of the labour inspectorates are likely to be sufficient to permit an effective control of the conditions of health and safety at work.

The main principles of European *labour law* are already implemented in the Czech legal system. However, adaptations are still necessary. A new Labour Code is under preparation, which seeks to bring Czech law fully into line with the *acquis* in the areas of protection of employees in case of insolvency of the employer and collective redundancies. On transfer of undertakings, information of employees on the conditions applicable to the employment relationship and on working time, there is a need for minor adaptations. The information and consultation of workers as requested by a number of EC Directives must be further developed.

Concerning *equal opportunity*, the basic provisions of EC non-discrimination law *between women and men* are covered.

Concerning the right to the free movement of workers, there would appear to be no obstacles to prevent the Czech Republic from being able to implement the provisions of the *acquis* in this area. The introduction of the right to free movement will however require changes in the national law, particularly as regards access to employment and a treatment free from discrimination on grounds of nationality.

In the field of *social security for migrant workers* accession does not, in principle, pose major problems, although certain technical adaptations will be necessary. More important is the administrative capacity to apply the detailed co-ordination rules in co-operation with other countries. The Czech Republic appears to have many of the administrative structures required to carry out these tasks, but further preparation and training will be necessary before the accession.

The two EC directives on the *warning labelling of cigarettes packages* and the *maximum tar content* have not yet been transposed into national law. An amendment to an existing Czech National Council Act is under consideration which would comply with EC requirements.

Conclusion

Provided the Czech Republic pursues its efforts, both in terms of adoption and of application of the EU *acquis*, the Czech Republic is likely to be able to take on the obligations of EC membership in the social area in the medium term.

Regional Policy and Cohesion

In accordance with Title XIV of the Treaty, the Community supports the strengthening of cohesion, mainly through the Structural Funds. The Czech Republic will have to implement these instruments effectively whilst respecting the principles, objectives and procedures which will be in place at the time of its accession.

The Europe Agreement provides for co-operation on regional development and spatial planning, notably through the exchange of information between local, regional and national authorities and the exchange of civil servants and experts.

The White Paper contains no specific provisions.

Descriptive Summary

In 1995, the Czech GDP/capita amounted to 55% of the EU average. The national unemployment rate stood at 3-4%. The unemployment rate is expected to increase somewhat in the coming years as a result of the necessary restructuring of large privatised companies. Looking at the regional unemployment rates shows that although comparatively low in all parts of the Czech Republic, important disparities exist between the most affected region (Most — Northern Bohemia: 7,2%) and the best performing region (Prague: 0,4%).

Currently, the Czech republic has no regional policy. Indeed, regional development initiatives are implemented through sectoral policies at national level. Economically weak areas are selected annually on the basis of principally unemployment rates. In 1996, for example, the chosen area covered 18,4% of the population of the Czech Republic.

A Ministry for Regional Development has recently been established. There exists no elected body between the State and the communes although the constitution foresees the establishment of the so-called territorial units of self-administration. At district level (77 units), the authorities are bodies of state administration with general competencies (no self government).

6 233 self governing municipalities are responsible for territorial development (town and country planning rather than local economic policy).

The Czech Republic's financial instruments at the disposal of regional development initiatives are limited. However, the share of total development related expenditure which could constitute counterpart funds to EC structural policy cannot yet be determined. Therefore, the Czech Republic's co-financing capacity cannot presently be evaluated with sufficient reliability.

Current and Prospective Assessment

The Czech Republic lacks an independent regional development policy. As mentioned above, regional development initiatives are implemented through the overall Czech development policy.

Since mid 1996, a more active approach to regional development has been adopted. The establishment of the Ministry of Regional Development will contribute to clarify responsibilities at government's level and possibly improve interministerial co-ordination.

Yet, Czech authorities still have to introduce important reforms to comply with EC's structural policies. Indeed, the Ministry of Regional Development has to insure proper co-ordination mechanisms at national level. Financial resources at the disposal of regional policy should be increased and efficient instruments need to be created. Finally, Czech authorities have to determine the future legal basis of a Czech regional policy in order to provide the appropriate legal structure for the actions envisaged to counteract regional disparities and for financing structural policy expenditure.

Conclusion

With the perspective of accession, the Czech Republic still needs to establish a legal, administrative and budgetary framework for an integrated regional policy and ensure its compliance with EU rules. Given the Czech Republic's administrative capacity and with the necessary political awareness, this should be achieved within a reasonable time-frame. Therefore, subject to the introduction of the necessary reforms, the Czech Republic should be able to, in the medium-term, apply the Community rules and channel effectively the funds from the EU structural policies.

3.6. Quality of Life and Environment

Environment

The Community's environmental policy, derived from the Treaty, aims towards sustainability based on the integration of environmental protection into EU sectoral policies, preventive action, the polluter pays principle, fighting environmental damage at the source, and shared responsibility. The *acquis* comprises approximately 200 legal acts covering a wide range of matters, including water and air pollution, management of waste and chemicals, biotechnology, radiation protection, and nature protection. Member States are required to ensure that an environmental impact assessment is carried out before development consent is granted for certain public and private projects.

The Europe Agreement stipulates that Czech development policies shall be guided by the principle of sustainable development and should fully incorporate environmental considerations. It also identifies environment as a priority for bilateral co-operation, as well as an area for approximation legislation to that of the Community.

The White Paper covers only a small part of the environmental *acquis*, namely product-related legislation, which is directly related to the free circulation of goods.

Descriptive Summary

In 1989, what is today the Czech Republic was one of the most polluted regions of Central Europe. Since then, however, the situation has improved considerably, as a result of the high level of environmental investment, but also due to industrial restructuring.

The main environmental challenge in the Czech Republic is air pollution. Though significant progress has been made (from 1989 to 1994, sulphur dioxide emissions fell by 36%, emissions of nitrogen oxides by 60% and particulate emissions by 49%), emissions of sulphur dioxides and nitrogen oxides remain high and require further measures in industry, transport and energy production. Uncontrolled landfill with hazardous and solid waste is another major problem inherited from the past. Problems in water quality are less urgent, but nonetheless very expensive to address. There are a number of industrial regions in decline which are particular environmental blackspots, most notably the Black Triangle and Ostrava.

Czech environmental legislation comprises a framework Environmental Protection Act of 1992 and numerous sectoral regulations, some of them dating back to the communist period. Policy priorities are set out in the State Environmental Policy approved in 1995, which comprises short-, middle- and long-term priorities. The Czech Republic makes extensive use of fiscal and economic instruments. The level of public environmental expenditure in terms of percentage of GDP exceeds the level in most of the EU Member States.

Whereas a number of basic environmental policies are in place, weaknesses in the Czech environmental system include inadequate enforcement and inefficiency of economic instruments by low level of fines, gaps in sectoral and subsidiary legislation covering implementation, and low environmental awareness and public participation.

Current and Prospective Assessment

Formal compliance with the EC *acquis* has progressed in recent years. The basic framework legislation is present but there are gaps in sectoral legislation and in secondary legislation governing economic instruments, implementation and enforcement. Particular attention should be given to the quick transposition of framework directives dealing with air, waste and water and the Integrated Pollution Prevention and Control (IPPC) directive, as well as the establishment of financing strategies for legislation in the water, air and waste sectors requiring major investments. Assuming that forthcoming acts (e.g. waste, chemicals and genetically modified organisms) are adopted according to legislative plans, formal compliance with the EC *acquis* will increase significantly over the coming few years.

The Czech Republic has adopted or is preparing legislation for most of the critical areas contained in the White Paper. Waste management is a somewhat neglected area at present but proposed legislation is focusing on plugging this gap.

Substantive compliance to the EC *acquis* is still low in certain areas, and the Czech Republic will need to focus on efficient implementation and enforcement, including efficiency of economic instruments. Important investment, both public and at enterprise level, will be needed. Accompanying mechanisms, such as licensing systems or public participation have to be established or improved and institutions involved in enforcement and implementation need to be reinforced. The country's environmental accession strategy should include implementation timetables for meeting the EC environmental *acquis* starting amongst others with implementation of the framework and IPPC directives mentioned above.

Conclusion

With present commitment maintained and existing levels of investment and provided planned legislation and the comprehensive environmental accession strategy are adopted and implemented, transposition of the whole environmental *acquis* as well as effective compliance with important elements of it (e.g. aspects of the air quality legislation, environmental impact assessment, industrial risks and chemicals legislation) should be achieved in the medium term. However, effective compliance with a number of pieces of legislation requiring a sustained high level of investment and considerable administrative effort (e.g. urban waste water treatment, drinking water, aspects of waste management and air pollution legislation) could be achieved only in the long term.

Consumer Protection

The Community *acquis* covers protection of the economic interests of consumers (including control of misleading advertisement, indication of prices, consumer credit, unfair contract terms, distance selling, package travel, sales away from business premises and timeshare property) as well as the general safety of goods and the specific sectors of cosmetics, textile names and toys.

The Europe Agreement provides for the harmonisation of legislation with Community law and co-operation with a view of achieving full compatibility between the systems of consumer protection in the Czech Republic and the Community.

Stage I measures of the White Paper focus on improving product safety, including cosmetics, textile names and toys, and on the protection of the economic interests of the consumer, notably measures on misleading advertising, consumer credit, unfair contract terms and indication of prices. Stage II measures relate to package travel, sales away from business premises and time-share property. New EC legislation which has been adopted recently (distance selling) or will be adopted soon (comparative advertising, price indication) will also need to be taken into account.

Descriptive Summary

An act on Consumer Protection was adopted in 1992 and amended in 1993 and 1995. There is no separate body in charge of consumer protection, and none appears to be planned. The overall responsibility for consumer affairs lies with the Ministry of Trade and Industry although other ministries or institutions also play an important if indirect role on consumer protection issues.

General consumer awareness is low. The consumer movement has been slow to develop, and there is no national organisation representing all Czech consumers. There are three active regional and local consumer groups.

Current and Prospective Assessment

On the protection of economic interests of consumers, the Czech legislation on the indication of prices is close to EC legislation, and a draft law is under preparation on consumer credit. But the approximation on misleading advertising is very incomplete compared to EU requirements.

The existing legislation on unfair contract terms would need to be substantially amended to cover the main subject matters of the EC Directive in this area. There is no legislation in a number of fields of importance to the consumer such as sales away from business premises, distance selling, package travel and timeshare property.

Most of the major EC concepts and obligations on general product safety and dangerous imitations have been incorporated into Czech legislation. In some cases Czech laws guarantee a better level of protection than EU standards but some important elements are missing. For the specific sectors, there is legislation on the textile names, and the first working proposal for a government regulation to implement the directive on the safety of toys is under preparation. The legislation on cosmetics is not in line with EC requirements yet but a new draft decree is underway.

The development of a strong and independent consumer movement, sustained by public authorities, will need to accompany the introduction of the *acquis*.

Conclusion

Considerable work on approximation is needed to bring Czech measures on consumer policy into line with the EC *acquis* in the medium term. Although there is a good degree of compatibility with EC standards in Czech priority areas such as the safety of goods, indication of prices and textile names, there are other sectors with no legislation. There is also a need to co-ordinate and organise the responsibilities of the different institutional bodies involved in consumer protection as well as to ensure the implementation of legislation.

3.7. Justice and Home Affairs

Present Provisions

The Justice and Home Affairs (JHA) *acquis* principally derives from the framework for cooperation set out in Title VI (Article K) of the Treaty on European Union (TEU), the 'third pillar', although certain 'first pillar' (EC Treaty) provisions and legislative measures are also closely linked.

The EU JHA framework primarily covers: asylum; control of external borders and immigration; customs cooperation and police cooperation against serious crime, including drug trafficking; and judicial cooperation on criminal and civil matters. The TEU stipulates key principles upon which such cooperation is based, notably the European Convention on Human Rights and the 1951 Geneva Convention on the Status of Refugees. It is also based implicitly on a range of international conventions concerning its fields of interest, notably those of the Council of Europe, the United Nations and the Hague Conference.

The legislative content of 'third pillar' *acquis* is different from the 'first pillar'; it consists of conventions, joint actions, joint positions and resolutions, (including the agreed elements of draft instruments which are in negotiation). A number of EU Conventions (including the 1990 Dublin Convention, and conventions relating to extradition, fraud and Europol) have been agreed by the Council and are now in the process of ratification by national Parliaments; several other conventions, including one on external frontiers are in various stages of negotiation in the Council. The JHA *acquis* involves a high degree of practical cooperation, as well as legislation and its effective implementation.

The New Treaty

For many of the above matters, the entry into force of the Treaty resulting from the Amsterdam Inter-Governmental Conference will mark the end of the current cooperation framework.

Reiterating the objective of developing the Union into an 'area of freedom, security and justice', the New Treaty brings these matters, including the free movement of persons, asylum and immigration, into the Community's sphere of competence.

On the free movement of persons in particular, the New Treaty provides for the incorporation of the Schengen *acquis* into the framework of the European Union and binds any candidate for EU membership to accept that *acquis* in full.

With regard to matters remaining within the cooperation framework, i.e. policing and criminal justice, the New Treaty provides for the reinforcement of the cooperation system.

The Europe Agreement and the White Paper

The Europe Agreement includes provision for cooperation in the fight against drug abuse and money laundering.

The White Paper does not deal directly with 'third pillar' subjects, but reference is made to 'first pillar' matters such as money laundering and freedom of movement of persons which are closely related to Justice and Home Affairs considerations. Reference is also made to the Brussels and Rome Conventions.

Descriptive Summary

General Preconditions for JHA Cooperation

The Czech Republic joined the Council of Europe in 1993 and has ratified the most important instruments concerning human rights. The Constitution provides for an independent judiciary according to the rule of law.

Institutional reform of JHA institutions is progressing satisfactorily. The Constitution guarantees data protection, but the Czech Republic's domestic legislation will need to be amended if it is to fully comply with Community requirements (see also separate section on the Single Market).

Asylum

The Czech Republic has ratified the Geneva Convention and the 1967 New York Protocol. The Charter of Fundamental Rights and Freedoms guarantees the right to asylum. Czech legislation and policy (inherited from the Czechoslovak Republic, dating from 1990) is currently being revised to bring the Czech Republic into line with EU standards including the principles of 'safe country of origin' and 'safe third country'. Asylum applications are handled by the Directorate of Aliens and Border Police Service of the Police Presidium. There were 2 100 asylum applicants in 1996, and some 1 200 temporary refugees from former Yugoslavia. New aliens legislation in preparation will cover legal provisions for granting temporary protection.

Immigration and Border Control

Since 1989 there has been a very large increase in the number of foreign nationals resident in the Czech Republic (now approximately 200 000). A current major priority for the Czech Government is to bring these migration flows under control. Residence and work permits are required for employment, but there are special rules for Slovaks given their close family and residence links with the Czech Republic. The Czech authorities are preparing new aliens legislation which will, among other things, stipulate that all visas must be issued abroad and also cover the registration of foreign nationals within the country. The Czech Republic is working to deal with expulsion of illegal immigrants in a structured manner, including seeking cooperation from IOM. Readmission agreements are in place with the Czech Republic's direct neighbours as well as Hungary, Romania, Canada and France. It is working to bring border management systems up to EU standards, but is hampered by the lack of technical equipment to check machine-readable documents and the fact that its internal communication system is not compatible with international norms.

Police Cooperation

Organised crime exists in the Czech Republic in the fields of trafficking of arms, explosives and nuclear materials, trafficking in women, prostitution, money laundering, tax fraud, and smuggling of stolen vehicles; violence and extortion are used. Specialised drugs and organised crime units have been established in the police force to tackle these crimes more effectively. The legal framework for tackling organised crime is being revised and strengthened. The Czech Republic has ratified the money laundering convention and domestic legislation is also in place (see also separate section on the Single Market). The Czech Republic experiences no specific threat from terrorism, but the Government has taken preventive action to bar entry to, and detain, suspected international terrorists.

Drugs

The Czech Republic is a transit country for drug trafficking. Domestic demand is significant. Quantities of heroin, cocaine and amphetamines have been seized in recent years. The Czech Republic has ratified the main international drugs conventions. Domestic anti-drugs legislation is largely in place, with a new law on drug precursors currently in preparation (manufacture, import and sale of drugs are criminal offences). Anti-drugs units have been established in the police and customs and are obtaining some good results. A National Anti-Drugs Policy has been in place since 1993, bringing together all relevant public and private bodies to tackle drug abuse and trafficking within the country. This is coordinated by the National Drugs Commission.

Judicial Cooperation

The judiciary is being prepared for EU accession. In general the level of expertise and efficiency of the court system is relatively low. Steps are being taken to upgrade them, but substantial efforts remain necessary. The Czech Republic has signed or ratified the main international criminal conventions in the field of judicial cooperation and is putting in place domestic measures to operate these conventions. On the civil side it has ratified very few conventions (maintenance and taking of evidence). The Czech Republic is planning to apply for accession to the Lugano Convention.

Current and Prospective Assessment

There are some important gaps still to be filled in the Czech Republic's legislation but for the most part the legislation is either in place or in preparation. An important priority for the near future will be improving communication systems in the field of border management, and bringing migration flows under control. It will also be important to maintain and develop effective systems for combating organised crime.

The main institutional problems lie in the field of resource constraints, the lack of expertise with new legislation in the police and judiciary, and the impact of institutional corruption. The Government is taking active steps to prepare the institutions for participation in the JHA process. The Czech Republic already has in place a small core of officials who are gaining experience of cooperation with EU countries and it can be expected that this capacity will develop further in the coming years.

Conclusion

The Czech Republic is likely to meet the justice and home affairs *acquis* (present and future) within the next few years, assuming progress continues at the current rate. The judiciary and police require particular attention, as well as the evolution of the Czech Republic's efforts to combat drugs and organised crime.

3.8. External Policies

Trade and International Economic Relations

The *acquis* in this field is made up principally of the Community's multilateral and bilateral commercial policy commitments, and its autonomous commercial defence instruments.

The Europe Agreement includes provisions in several areas requiring parties to act in accordance with WTO/ GATT principles, or other relevant international obligations.

The White Paper includes no provisions in this field.

Descriptive Summary

The Czech Republic has developed an open, trading economy and is a member of the World Trade Organisation (WTO). Upon accession the Czech Republic would have to comply with the obligations of the plurilateral WTO agreements to which the Community is a party.

At present the Czech Republic does not maintain quantitative restrictions on any textile or clothing products. On accession the Community textiles policy would be extended to the Czech Republic; any Community restrictions still maintained at the date of accession would require adjustment by an appropriate amount to take account of Czech accession.

Current and Prospective Assessment

On accession the Czech Republic would have to apply the Community's Common Customs Tariff, and the external trade provisions of the Common Agricultural Policy. The post Uruguay Round weighted average levels of most favoured nation duties for industrial products will be 3,8% for the Czech Republic and 3,6% for the Community.

In its relations with international organisations, the Czech Republic should ensure that its actions and commitments respect the Europe Agreement and ensure a harmonious adoption of its future obligations as a member of the Community.

On accession the Czech Republic would become party to the Community's various preferential agreements. Preferential agreements between the Czech Republic and third countries would, in general, have to be terminated on accession.

In the area of trade in services and establishment the Czech Republic has already made good progress, and it should be possible to resolve any remaining, significant inconsistencies between the commitments of the Czech Republic and those of the Community.

In April 1997 the Czech Republic introduced an import deposit scheme for a large number of consumer products, which is not in conformity with the Europe Agreement. This scheme should be withdrawn.

On accession the Czech Republic would have to repeal national legislation in the field of commercial defence instruments, and EC legislation would become applicable there.

Experience from previous accessions has shown that the automatic extension of existing anti-dumping measures to new Member States prompts third countries to raise problems in terms of the compatibility of this approach with relevant WTO provisions. It has also shown that accession creates a potential for circumventing measures adopted by the Community under the commercial defence instruments. This happens when, prior to accession, substantial quantities of the products subject to measures are exported to the territory of the future Member State and, on accession, are automatically released for free circulation in the enlarged customs territory. These two problems would have to be addressed during the Czech Republic's pre-accession phase.

The Czech Republic is a member of three out of four existing regimes for the non-proliferation of weapons of mass-destruction, and is a candidate for membership of the fourth. The Czech Republic's list of dual-use goods and technologies is presently being updated and is expected to correspond with the Community control list of dual-use items, enhanced by the chemicals items belonging to the regime of the Chemical Weapons Convention. Arms export is also controlled. The Czech Republic should have no problems applying EC legislation in this field.

Conclusion

The Czech Republic is well placed to be able to meet Community requirements in this field in the medium term, provided they reinforce their efforts to eliminate existing trade barriers in order to align themselves more closely with the Community trade regime.

Development

The *acquis* in the development sector is made up principally of the Lomé Convention, which runs until early 2000.

Neither the Europe Agreement or the White Paper include provisions in this field.

Descriptive Summary

The Czech Republic has no preferential trade agreements with ACP countries. However, under its GSP scheme, the Czech Republic grants preferential treatment in the form of reduced duties to a number of ACP countries, and grants duty free access to those ACP countries considered as Least Developed Countries.

The Czech Republic has a modest but well established system of development aid which falls into two basic categories: development aid and humanitarian aid. Development aid is provided both bilaterally (20,25 million US $ in 1996), and multilaterally (through voluntary contributions to the UN bodies as well as to the World Bank, including the International Development Association, and the IMF).

Current and Prospective Assessment

On accession, the Czech Republic should apply its preferential trade regime to the ACP States and participate, together with the other Member States, in financing the European Development Fund (EDF), which provides financial aid under the Lomé Convention.

Applying the Lomé trade regime should not generally be a source of difficulties for the Czech Republic.

Normally, new Member States accede to the Lomé Convention by means of a protocol on the date of their accession to the EU.

Conclusion

The Czech Republic is well placed to be able to meet EU requirements in this field in the next few years.

Customs

The *acquis* in this sector is the Community Customs Code and its implementing provisions; the EC's Combined Nomenclature; the Common Customs Tariff including trade preferences, tariff quotas and tariff suspensions; and other customs-related legislation outside the scope of the customs code.

The Europe Agreement covers the establishment of a free trade area with the Community and the progressive removal of customs duties on a wide range of products, according to clear timetables starting from the date of entry into force of the agreement.

The White Paper includes in Stage I, measures to consolidate and streamline the free trade established under the Europe Agreement, including legislation compatible with the Customs Code, Combined Nomenclature, etc. Stage II concerns the adoption of the full Community legislation, with a view to joining the customs union upon accession.

Descriptive Summary

On accession the Czech customs authorities would be required to assume all the responsibilities necessary for the protection and control of their part of the EU's external border. (Whether the Czech Republic would be responsible for the EU's external land frontier would depend on which other countries acceded at the same time). Besides the provisions on indirect taxation, the Czech customs authorities would be responsible for the implementation and enforcement at the external border of the Community's common commercial policy, the common agricultural policy, the common fisheries policy, etc.

The Czech Republic's capacity fully to apply the *acquis* presupposes the possibility to adopt and implement the Community legislation; and the existence of an adequate level of infrastructure and equipment, in particular in terms of computerisation and investigation means and the establishment of an efficient customs organisation with a sufficient number of qualified and motivated staff showing a high degree of integrity.

With the support of the technical assistance provided by customs programmes, the Czech Republic has achieved almost full compatibility of the Czech customs legislation to the Community's customs code.

The Czech Republic has aligned its national goods nomenclature to the Community's Combined Nomenclature as of 1 January 1996. In addition, a Czech Integrated Tariff already exists. This will greatly facilitate the comparison of the Czech tariff rates with the Common Customs Tariff rates. The Czech Republic also operates a Binding Tariff Information System similar to the one applied in the Community.

The Czech Republic adopted on 1 January 1997 the new system of cumulation of origin between European countries.

The Czech Republic became a contracting party to the EC/EFTA Common Transit Convention and to the Convention on Simplification of Formalities on 1 July 1996.

Current and Prospective Assessment

The Czech Republic would need to adapt its national procedures to the Community legislation regarding suspensive arrangements and customs procedures with economic impact. At the moment of accession, some technical transitional arrangements would be needed, notably for operations beginning before the date of accession but which are concluded after that date.

The import deposit scheme operated by the Czech Republic is a measure having equivalent effect to a quantitative restriction. Consequently this scheme should be abolished as soon as possible.

Tax-free shops at land borders have been allowed by the Czech republic since 1991 under national legislation. At the moment there are six duty-free shops at land borders with Germany and ten duty-free shops at land borders with Austria. These shops are not allowed at land borders inside the EC territory, therefore the abolition of this kind of facility would be a condition for accession. The Czech authorities should accelerate the dismantling of these shops as soon as possible.

It will be important that the Czech customs authorities can participate appropriately in the various computerised systems necessary for the management, in the customs union/internal market, of the customs and indirect tax provisions, as well as the computerised systems for mutual administrative assistance in customs, agricultural and indirect tax matters.

The Czech Republic would need on accession to dismantle customs controls at the borders with EU Member States and with other acceding countries. The resources which could be needed for the reinforcement of the border posts along the external land frontiers which the Czech Republic may have with non-EU Member States should be taken it into account in its strategic planning.

Finally, a potential for a problem exists arising from the customs union between the Czech Republic and Slovakia, in the event that these two countries do not accede simultaneously to the Community.

Conclusion

The Czech Republic is making a major effort to align its organisation and staff to the duties that have to be carried out by a modern customs administration.

If it reinforces its efforts, particularly in relation to project management in the computerisation area, the Czech Republic should be ready to fulfil the responsibilities of an EC customs administration within the next few years.

Common Foreign and Security Policy

Since 1989, the foreign and security policy of the Czech Republic (prior to 1993, Czechoslovakia) has been reoriented towards European and Euro-Atlantic integration. The Czech Republic has been an active participant in the dialogue arrangements provided for under the Union's Common Foreign and Security Policy and whenever invited has supported EU actions within that framework.

The Czech Republic is a member of the UN, OSCE, Council of Europe and many other international organisations. It is an associate partner of WEU, participates in the NACC, the PfP and has made clear its desire to become a member of the WEU and NATO as soon as possible; it has been invited to open negotiations for membership of NATO. It has sent troops to participate in IFOR/SFOR. It also participates in a number of regional organisations including CEFTA and the CEI, although it does not favour further institutionalisation of regional co-operation.

There are no territorial disputes between the Czech Republic and any Member State of the Union. Neither does it have any territorial or other disputes with neighbouring associated countries. The Czech Republic, largely within the framework of the Stability Pact, has signed with all neighbouring countries new treaties in respect of state frontiers or negotiated the succession in respect of existing treaties. There remain some minor issues to be settled with the Slovak Republic.

The Czech Republic has a sizeable diplomatic service which would permit it as a member of the Union to play a significant role. It maintains 89 representations abroad and employs 785 diplomatic staff.

The Czech Republic supports non-proliferation of nuclear, biological and chemical weapons and is a signatory to all relevant international agreements. It exercises strict control concerning the dual use of technology, being a member or candidate member of all the major existing export control regimes. The Czech armed forces, which are under democratic control, are being reorganised to meet NATO requirements. The defence industrial base has suffered from a number of major problems and is also in the process of re-organisation.

The Czech Government has confirmed to the Commission that it is ready and able to participate fully and actively in the Common Foreign and Security Policy.

The assessment of Czech foreign and security policy to date leads to the expectation that as a member it could effectively fulfil its obligations in this field.

3.9. Financial Questions

Financial Control

The implementation of Community policies, especially for agriculture and the Structural Funds, requires efficient management and control systems for public expenditure, with provisions to fight fraud. Approximation of legislation is moreover needed to allow the system of 'own resources' to be introduced, with satisfactory provision for accounting.

The Europe Agreement provides for cooperation in audit and financial control, including technical assistance from the Community as appropriate.

The White Paper includes no measures in this field.

Descriptive Summary

The Supreme Audit Office (SAO) which has existed since 1993 is an independent external control authority, answerable only to Parliament (which nominates the president and vice-president). The SAO is responsible for controlling the management of state assets and the state budget. It provides an opinion on the draft of the state closing account submitted annually by the Government to Parliament and on the quarterly budget reports. The model of control used in the Czech Republic is based upon the principles of the Lima declaration adopted by the International Organisation of Supreme Audit Institutions.

The results of audits by the SAO — 'audit protocols' — are published in its bulletin and sent to Parliament, the Government (which should, if necessary, adopt remedial measures) and, upon request, the ministries audited. The SAO is entitled to request that corrective measures be taken to be made by the controlled subject, but has no power to impose any sanctions (exception disciplinary fines for non-cooperation during audit).

With regard to the future control of Community funds, it is intended that the necessary staffing and training will take place to ensure effective external control by the SAO in relation to all Community programmes. It is also foreseen that the jurisdiction of control bodies will cover controls of financial regularity, legality and sound financial management.

The ministry of Finance is the central body in the state administration responsible for internal controls over the state budget, taxes, fees and customs duties, financial control and foreign exchange issues and prices. The ministry is preparing to enlarge its expenditure control capacities.

The financial control carried out by the state administration is performed by territorial financial bodies (financial offices and financial directorates), subordinated to the Ministry of Finance, which carry out financial checks on the subsidies granted from the state budget and specific tax collection and control activities.

Each minister and manager of each budgetary chapter is responsible for the management and control of the revenue and expenditure operations taking place within their jurisdiction, including that all activities are legal and follow approved regulations.

With regard to fraud, the Czech Republic has no central authority responsible for fighting fraud. However, it is within the competence of the Czech customs authorities, at all levels, to combat fraud (in court criminal proceedings they have the status of a police authority).

The Police Service for Corruption Detection and Serious Economic Offences is responsible for combating financial fraud both on a national and international level — their activities cover three essential areas: a) corruption in the government and local government; b) money laundering; c) serious economic offences (especially cases of abuse of financial funds).

Current and Prospective Assessment

Main parts of the Czech financial control system have been put in place only recently — e.g. the Supreme Audit Office was created in 1993.

Further development of financial control is necessary.

The current system of internal financial control in the Czech Republic does not correspond to the provisions foreseen by the EC for each Member State. However, the Government has expressed its intention to improve its budgetary control.

External control — done above all by the Supreme Audit Office — seems to be well in place.

Article 84 of the Europe Agreement which states that an internal control unit is to be established within each organisation has not been sufficiently implemented. No special regulation has yet been enacted to provide for independent, ex-ante control in the Czech Republic.

Concerning 'own resources' the application of Regulation (EEC) No 913/92 does not seem to be problematic for the Czech Republic. Further cooperation with the Commission will be needed on the compatibility of Czech provisions with Regulation (EEC) No 1552/89.

For the issue of fraud there is a need to ensure an appropriate staffing level and a unified information system for the exchange of information.

Conclusion

The financial control system in the Czech Republic is just being developed. Major elements to control the allocation and use of public resources are not yet in place. However, if the necessary resources are made available, the Czech Republic should be in a position in the medium term to fulfil the EC requirements.

Budgetary Implications

The communication entitled 'Agenda2000' sets out the overall financial framework which should accommodate the budget impact of any future enlargements in the medium term. This is to ensure that any enlargement is compatible with proposed Community policy guidelines within reasonable budget limits.

As things stand, it would be difficult, not to say premature, to attempt precise country-by-country evaluations of the budgetary implications of each of the applicants joining the Union. Exactly what the impact would be may vary considerably depending on a whole series of factors:

☐ the date on which the applicant country joins;

☐ developments in Community policies between now and then, in particular the decisions to be taken on further reform of the common agricultural policy and new guidelines for structural measures;

☐ the progress made by the applicant countries in terms of growth, increasing their competitiveness and productivity and their ability to absorb the *acquis;*

☐ the transitional measures that will come out of the negotiations.

Only a few orders of magnitude for certain budget categories and an overall estimate can be given purely as a guide.

Expenditure

If the common agricultural policy were to be reformed along the lines suggested by the Commission, once the reforms were fully up and running and in terms of just market intervention measures, the Czech Republic's accession would give rise to additional expenditure of around 1 to 2 % in relation to likely expenditure on the present fifteen Member States.

After a phasing-in period, the allocations for the Czech Republic under structural activities would top around 4 % of GNP.

Application of the other internal Community policies in the new member countries would be likely to involve additional expenditure probably in excess of their relative proportion of Union GNP, since for certain policies the additional implementing costs also depend on the target population, the geographical area covered or the number of Member States involved in the coordination and harmonisation measures. The GNP of the Czech Republic is currently 0,7 % of total Union GNP.

By contrast, the Czech Republic's accession should not involve significant additional expenditure as far as Union external action is concerned.

It should not be forgotten that when an applicant country joins, the Community budget will no longer have to bear the costs of grants the country was eligible for under the various pre-accession programmes, such as PHARE.

In light of the above, the estimated costs in the three areas mentioned arising from the Czech Republic's accession should fall within the range of, annually, 2,6 and 3,3 billion ECU in 2005-2006 (at constant 1997 prices).

Revenue

Assuming full application of the own resources system, the new members' contributions to the Community budget should, in terms of total GNP and VAT resources (taking account of the capping rules applying to VAT), be close to the proportion of the Union's GNP they account for, which in the Czech Republic's case is around 0,7 %. The Czech Republic's portion of traditional own resources will depend on the structure of its trade flows at the time of accession.

To ensure that the own resources are established, monitored and made available in line with Community regulations, the Czech Republic will have to overhaul its current customs system. In addition, for the purposes of accurately calculating the GNP resource considerable improvements will have to be made to the national accounts to ensure that they are reliable, homogeneous and complete. Improving the statistics will also be essential for drawing up the VAT own resources base, which will mean bringing the Czech Republic's VAT system fully into line with the Community directives.

4. Administrative Capacity to apply the *Acquis*

The European Council in Madrid in December 1995 concluded that the harmonious integration into the EU of the Central and Eastern European applicant States would, in particular, require the adjustment of their administrative structures. This chapter examines the current state of the public administration in the Czech Republic, including relevant aspects of the judicial system, and assesses the current and prospective ability to carry out the functions required of it in a modern, democratic state, with a particular focus on the need to administer matters related to the *acquis*.

4.1. Administrative Structures

A description of Czech Republic constitutional structures, their powers and responsibilities, including those of regional and local government, is given in Chapter 1.

At the central level there are 14 ministries and 8 so-called state administrative bodies (such as the Statistical Office, the Czech National Bank, etc.). The Government Committee for European Integration, headed by the Prime Minister, is the central coordinating body for EU accession related matters.

A draft civil-service law was elaborated between 1992 and 1995 and discussed in Parliament. Because of lack of agreement between the major parties, however, it has not yet been adopted. There are no set rules for recruitment or promotion.

On the whole the civil service is politically independent. The position of Deputy Minister, in effect the highest official level, is usually filled with persons who have a party affiliation.

The total number of people employed by state bodies is estimated at about 250 000, which includes 40 000 police and 30 000 military. The Government's economic policy packages of April and May 1997 foresee significant cuts in the state budget. These are expected to affect the number of persons employed by the state. Salaries in the private sector are on average three times higher than those in the public sector.

Since 1990 consecutive Czech(oslovak) Governments have given low priority to the necessary reform and modernisation of the public administration. There are no indications that this position is changing.

In 1994 a Government Committee for European Integration was established. In this framework, each ministry has set up a unit responsible for EU matters (see also the section of the Introduction concerning relations between the European Union and the Czech Republic).

4.2. Administrative and Judicial Capacity

Czechoslovakia was administered under central planning during the communist period. The communist system rejected the primacy of the rule of law and subjugated the law and the administration to the implementation of Party policy. Against this background, both the administration and the rule of law itself increasingly came to be seen by the public as instruments of political control.

The structures of the public administration are, however, broadly similar to those existing in many EU Member States. Some important structural weaknesses exist, most notably the lack of a central department with general oversight of the civil service (the Office of Legislation and the civil service (the Office of Legislation and Public Service was disbanded after the last elections in the Czech Republic): this can lead to inefficiencies and lack of standardisation or well developed strategy in areas such as training.

Despite problems which need to be addressed, the process of government proceeds adequately much of the time. At the higher levels the quality of officials has greatly improved. However, in most ministries the units responsible for legal administration are poorly staffed. There is also a shortage of able and experienced staff in areas such as banking supervision and capital markets, and implementation and enforcement structures in areas such as environmental policy require further strengthening.

The political independence of the civil service, while not as firmly entrenched as would ideally be the case, is sufficiently well established as to provide a fair degree of reassurance that the functions of public administration can be carried out in a non-partisan manner (see also Chapter 1, concerning the lustration law). However, the lack of an adequate legal basis for the civil service is a significant problem which requires early resolution if the role and function of the civil service is to be adequately guaranteed.

Some key ministries, including the Ministry of Foreign Affairs, show signs of under-staffing. The availability of better paid work in the private sector has led to a significant number of able people leaving the civil service. However, this has been much less the case at the lower levels of the public administration, so overall figures for staff-turnover are not particularly high. Nonetheless, clearly the loss of able staff is to the detriment of the public administration's ability effectively to function.

Public confidence in the civil service is affected negatively by the legacy of the past, since a significant number of the civil servants worked under the communist regime. Possible abuses of power, are not a major current factor affecting public confidence in the civil service. Corruption is present in the system and may be increasing.

The lack of any substantial or coherent plan for public administration modernisation is the single greatest cause for concern in this field. Such measures as have been taken are thoroughly inadequate in the face of the important problems which require resolution. In addition to the points already outlined a wide ranging reform process will need to be instigated and sustained if the Czech Republic is to establish a civil service of the overall quality, level of training, motivation and flexibility required on the country's path to further economic and social development, and membership of the EU.

As far as EU matters specifically are concerned, the development and reinforcement of a central coordinating structure in this area will be of great importance to the Czech Republic's ability successfully to handle the demands placed on it in the pre-accession period and beyond.

Key Areas for the Implementation of the *Acquis*

The uniform application of EC law: the effective application of the *acquis* presupposes that the judicial authorities of Member States are able to apply the provisions of the Treaty dealing with ensuring the unity and application of the *acquis*, and are able to ensure the proper functioning of the Single Market and Community policies in general. A high quality and well trained and resourced judiciary is necessary for the application by the courts of EC law, including cases of direct effect, and cases of referral to the European Court of Justice under the terms of Article 177 of the Treaty.

The judicial system in the Czech Republic has weaknesses, concerning expertise and, to some extent, resources. A special, and reinforced, effort will have to be made with urgency if the system is to be able effectively to apply the *acquis* in the medium term.

Single market: the ability of the Czech Republic to ensure the correct application of Community requirements in the Single Market, particularly concerning the free movement of goods and services presupposes the existence of highly developed and effective regulatory, standardisation, certification and supervisory authorities, able to act fully in accordance with EC rules. An analysis of these points is made in Chapter 3.1 (under 'The Four Freedoms').

Concerning the administrative capacity in respect of free movement of goods, the situation in the Czech Republic is largely satisfactory. The Czech Office for Standards, Metrology and Testing has a staff of 60, which appears adequate, and of which the technical competence is sufficiently high. Questions remain, however, about the implementation of market surveillance, and the proper separation between the regulatory, standardisation and certification functions. Concerning the free movement of services, the situation is not yet satisfactory. The Czech National Bank is responsible for banking supervision and has a staff of 86. However, developments in the banking sector over the past few years point to the need for more effective supervision. The semi-independent Securities Office's technical competence requires significant improvement. It has a staff of 65 with few possessing the necessary knowledge or skills. Technical equipment is, however, of good quality. The supervisory body for the insurance sector has a staff of 16, presenting it with an almost impossible task in attempting to cope with it responsibilities in the present insurance market.

In order to meet EU requirements in this area some important improvements will still be required.

Competition: as explained in Chapter 3.1 (under 'Competition') enforcement of competition law requires the establishment of anti-trust and state aid monitoring authorities, and that the judicial system, the public administration and the relevant economic operators have a sufficient understanding of competition law and policy.

In the Czech Republic the central authority is the Office for the Protection of Economic Competition which has 90 staff; this is adequate. The level of expertise is good. The administrative structures already exist effectively to implement EU requirements in this field.

Telecommunications: in order to formulate and implement the many liberalisation regulations contained in the *acquis* in this field it is necessary to have a regulatory and policy making body that is effectively separated from any operating company.

In the Czech Republic this body is the Czech Telecommunications Office, which is to be separated from the Transport Ministry. It is well staffed and functioning, although the regulatory department should be strengthened.

Indirect taxation: the effective administration of the indirect taxation *acquis* presupposes structures capable of implementing the EC legislation concerning the harmonisation of Valued Added Tax and excise duties in an environment in which fiscal controls at internal EU frontiers have been abolished; and the excise system is based on the tax warehouses, duty being payable at the local rate in the Member State at the time the goods are consumed. This requires a highly developed and well trained and resourced service, with a high degree of integrity.

In the Czech Republic the relevant authority is the Ministry of Finance with a total of 14 000 staff (for the financial and tax administration, including customs). Due to a large turnover of staff, resulting partly from trained staff being recruited by the private sector, it is difficult to estimate the capacities of existing staff. In order to ensure the effective administration of the *acquis* in this area it will be necessary to consolidate and improve the overall professional standards of the staff, including training measures and improvements in pay.

Agriculture: the administrative requirements in the agricultural area primarily concern veterinary and phytosanitary control, to protect public health and ensure the free movement of agricultural goods; and the ability to administer the mechanisms and requirements of the CAP, including high standards of financial control and official statistics. These points are dealt with in Chapter 3.4 (under 'Agriculture'); general standards in the statistical field are examined in Chapter 3.3 (under 'Statistics').

Concerning the administrative capacity in respect of veterinary and phytosanitary controls, the situation in the Czech Republic is largely satisfactory. There is a well established infrastructure for veterinary control and inspection. But testing and inspection facilities need to be upgraded. The Agriculture and Foodstuffs Inspection employs 412 staff, but has recruitment difficulties. The State Veterinary Inspection employs 1 700 staff. Concerning the administration of general CAP requirements, the appropriate administrative structures need further development.

In order to meet EC requirements in this area, some improvements are still required, but much has already been achieved.

Transport: the application of the EC internal market and competition requirements to the transport sector, the development of relevant infrastructure products, and other aspects of the transport *acquis* will present administrative challenges to new Member States.

The responsible government authority in the Czech Republic is the Ministry of Transport and Communications. The number of staff is not currently available to the Commission. Though the administration has taken steps to improve its functioning, there are still problems arising from a lack of qualified staff. This raises particular concerns with regard to enforcement of safety controls.

Employment and social policy: a central administrative requirement in respect of the *acquis* in this area is adequate inspection capacity, particularly concerning health and safety at work.

In the Czech Republic the labour inspectorate requires considerable reinforcement of staff resources and expertise.

Regional policy and cohesion: the main administrative requirements in this area are the existence of appropriate and effective administrative bodies, and in particular a high degree of competence and integrity in the administration of Community funds.

In the Czech Republic the principal administrative body is the Ministry for Regional Development. The number of staff employed is not currently available to the Commission. The creation of the ministry has helped start a process of greater coordination. The situation concerning financial control is not yet satisfactory, but is progressing reasonably well (see the section, below on 'Financial control'). The effective administration of the *acquis* in this area will require further development of the institutional and administrative framework.

Environment: because EC environmental policy, involves the integration of environmental protection into EC sectoral policies the administrative requirement is potentially very wide, affecting many bodies not normally associated with environmental protection. However, the main responsibility lies with environment ministries and various subsidiary bodies.

In the Czech Republic the Environment Ministry employs 460 staff. Monitoring is carried out by sectoral authorities and enforcement is carried out by the ministries and 9 regional inspectorates. These arrangements are not yet adequate. The effective administration of the *acquis* in this area will require these institutions to be reinforced.

Consumer protection: in this area, the effective administration of the *acquis* requires the allocation of overall responsibility to a specific state body through which the formulation, implementation and enforcement of consumer policy and consumer protection legislation can be undertaken.

In the Czech Republic the Ministry of Trade and Industry has authority to develop and implement consumer protection policy. As regards non-governmental consumer bodies these remain too weak in the Czech Republic. There remains confusion about the exact scope and objectives of consumer policy. This in part explains difficulties in the effective enforcement of consumer laws; however, other factors which need to be addressed include a lack of expert staff, organisational deficits, and a lack of sensitivity to consumer questions among the judiciary.

Justice and home affairs: oversight of justice and home affairs questions falls to justice and interior ministries. The administrative structures need to be able to deal effectively with asylum and migration questions, border management, police cooperation and judicial cooperation. There is an overriding need for sufficient and properly trained staff with a high degree of integrity.

In the Czech Republic the justice and interior ministries are not adequately staffed in all areas. The capacity to handle asylum and migration questions is not yet assured through the Directorate of Aliens and Border Police, but is being brought into line with EU standards. Border management is also being brought up to EU standards, but is hampered by procedural problems and lack of equipment. Specialist police units to tackle organised crime have been established, and cooperation with other countries is improving. The court system, however, lacks expertise and efficiency, although judicial cooperation is generally good. The effective administration of the *acquis* in this area will require improvement of communications for border management, increased financial and human resources (especially specialist training), and taking steps to combat corruption.

Customs: applying the *acquis* in this area requires an adequate level of infrastructure and equipment, including computerisation and investigation resources, and the establishment of an efficient customs organisation with a sufficient number of qualified and motivated staff showing a high degree of integrity.

In the Czech Republic the customs service employs 8 400 staff. Due to a high turnover of staff, it is difficult to estimate their efficiency, and therefore the adequacy of staffing levels. The effective administration of the *acquis* in this area will require improvements to technical equipment, and retention of qualified and experienced staff.

Financial control: the protection of the Community's financial interests requires the development of anti-fraud services, training of specialised staff (investigators, magistrates) and the reinforcement of systems of specific cooperation. The implementation of Community policies, especially for agriculture and the Structural Funds, requires efficient management and control systems for public expenditure, with provisions to fight fraud. Administratively it is essential to have a clear separation between external and internal control. Police and judicial authorities need to be able effectively to handle complex transnational financial crime (including fraud, corruption and money laundering) which could affect the Community's financial interests.

In the Czech Republic the main external control body is the Supreme Audit Office which has 490 staff. The effective administration of the *acquis* in this area will require considerable further development of the systems in place, but this should be possible assuming that the necessary resources are made available.

4.3. General Evaluation

The Czech Republic's administrative structures will require a significant and sustained effort of reform if there is to be adequate capacity in the medium term effectively to administer the *acquis*.

A definite evaluation at this stage of the ability of the judicial system in the Czech Republic effectively to apply Community law in the medium term is difficult, although it is clear that efforts of reform are required.

C — Summary and Conclusion

The Czech Republic submitted its application for membership of the European Union on 17 January 1996. Its request is part of the historic process of ending the division of Europe and consolidating the establishment of democracy across the continent.

In accordance with the provisions of Article O of the Treaty, the Commission has, at the request of the Council, prepared an opinion on the Czech Republic's request for membership.

The Czech Republic's preparation for membership is going forward notably on the basis of the *Europe Agreement* which entered into force on 1 February 1995. Implementation of the *White Paper* of May 1995 on the internal market, another essential element of the pre-accession strategy, is going ahead on the basis of a Plan agreed by the government in the spring of 1996. The government has put in place the necessary mechanisms to coordinate its policies for European integration.

In preparing its opinion, the Commission has applied the *criteria established at the Copenhagen European Council* of June 1993. The conclusions of this Council stated that those candidate countries of Central and Eastern Europe who wish to do so shall become members of the Union if they meet the following conditions:

☐ stability of institutions guaranteeing democracy, the rule of law, human rights and respect for and protection of minorities;

☐ the existence of a functioning market economy, as well as the ability to cope with competitive pressures and market forces within the Union;

☐ the ability to take on the obligations of membership, including adherence to the aims of political, economic and monetary union.

A judgment on these three groups of criteria – political, economic, and the ability to take on the *acquis* — depends also on the capacity of a country's administrative and legal systems to put into effect the principles of democracy and the market economy and to apply and enforce the *acquis* in practice.

The *method* followed in preparing theseopinions has been to analyse the situation in each candidate country, looking forward to the medium term prospects, and taking into account progress accomplished and reforms already under way. For the political criteria, the Commission has analysed the current situation, going beyond a formal account of the institutions to examine how democracy and the rule of law operate in practice.

*

* *

1) Political Criteria

The Czech Republic's political institutions function properly and in conditions of stability. They respect the limits on their competences and cooperate with each other. Legislative elections in 1992 and 1996 were free and fair. The Opposition plays a normal part in the operation of the institutions. Efforts to improve the operation of the judiciary and to intensify the fight against corruption must be sustained.

There are no major problems over respect for fundamental rights. There are, however, some weaknesses in laws governing freedom of the press. Particular attention will need to be paid to the conditions governing any further extension of a law excluding from public service members of the former security services and active members of the communist regime. There is a problem of discrimination affecting the Roma, notably through the operation of the citizenship law.

The Czech Republic presents the characteristics of a democracy, with stable institutions guaranteeing the rule of law, human rights, and respect for and protection of minorities.

2) Economic Criteria

After some disruption caused by the separation of the Czech and Slovak Republics in 1993, economic growth resumed in 1994 and has been strongly sustained since, though at a lower rate (4,0%) in 1996. The Czech Republic has maintained tight fiscal policies, but both trade and current account deficits grew in 1996. Inflation has gradually declined over recent years, and stood at 8,8% in 1996. GDP per head is about

55% of the EU average, for a population of 10,3 million. The agricultural sector employed 6% of the labour force in 1995, and accounted for 5% of Gross Value Added. The EU's share of Czech trade has risen from 27% in 1989 (as Czechoslovakia) to 55%.

On the basis of its analysis, the Commission's judgment as to the *Czech Republic's ability to meet the economic criteria* established at Copenhagen is as follows.

The Czech Republic can be regarded as a functioning *market economy*. Market mechanisms operate widely, and the role of the State in the economy has been completely changed. Substantial success has been achieved in stabilising the economy. Unemployment is among the lowest in Europe. However, as the recent emergence of macroeconomic imbalances has shown, further progress will need to be made over the next few years, notably in strengthening corporate governance and the financial system.

The Czech Republic should be able to cope with *competitive pressure* and *market forces* within the Union in the medium term, provided that change at the enterprise level is accelerated. The country benefits from a trained and skilled workforce, and infrastructure is relatively good. Investment in the economy has been high in recent years, with foreign direct investment also strong. The country has successfully reoriented its trade towards the West. But although the quality of exported goods is improving, their value added is still low. The banking sector is dominated by a few, partly state-owned banks and its competitive position is not strong. The main challenge for the Czech Republic is to press on with enterprise restructuring in order to improve the medium term performance of the economy and as a way of redressing the imbalances on the external side.

3) Capacity to take on the Obligations of Membership

The Czech Republic's ability to take on the *acquis* has been evaluated according to several indicators:

☐ the obligations set out in the Europe Agreement, particularly those relating to the right of establishment, national treatment, free circulation of goods, intellectual property and public procurement;

☐ implementation of the measures set out in the White Paper as essential for establishing the Single Market;

☐ progressive transposition of the other parts of the *acquis*.

The Czech Republic has already adopted significant elements of the provisions of the Europe Agreement, and according to the timetable for implementation set out in it. Few serious bilateral problems have arisen, though the Czech imposition in April 1997 of an import deposit scheme was not in conformity with the Agreement. The Czech Republic has achieved a satisfactory rate of transposition of the rules and directives identified in the White Paper, though there is still a considerable amount of legislative work left to do.

For most of the areas relating specifically to the *Single Market*, the legislative basis is more or less in place. In certain fields, particularly financial services and taxation, further work is still needed.

Notwithstanding the efforts which have been made, the real progress made in transposing legislation still needs to be accompanied by concrete measures of implementation, as well as establishment of an effective administrative underpinning. Overall, the administrative infrastructure is either well-established or recently set up and functioning normally. But substantial further efforts are needed.

As for the *other parts of the acquis*, the Czech Republic should not have difficulty in applying it from the date of accession in the following fields: education, training and youth; research and technological development; telecommunications; statistics; consumer protection; small and medium enterprises; trade and international economic relations; and development.

By contrast, substantial efforts will be needed for the Czech Republic to be able to apply the *acquis* in the fields of audio-visual, and customs (though efforts are under way in this sector).

Provided that past and current efforts at industrial restructuring and modernisation are continued, and reinforced in the case of heavy industries, most sectors of Czech *industry* should face no major problems to integrate into the Single Market in the medium term.

For the *environment*, very substantial efforts will be needed, including massive investment and strengthening of administrative capacity to enforce legislation. Partial compliance with the *acquis* could be achieved in the medium term. Full compliance could be achieved only in the long term.

For *transport*, the Czech Government has already made notable progress towards meeting the *acquis*. Efforts need to be pursued in respect of road freight transport. But meeting the *acquis* relating to the Single Market should not pose real problems. Investment will be needed to extend the European transport network so as to ensure that the Single Market functions well.

In order to apply the *employment* and *social affairs acquis* in the medium term, work is needed to adapt legislation in the field of health and safety at work.

In the field of *regional policy* and *cohesion*, if the Czech Republic works to establish the necessary administrative framework and achieve the substantial improvement needed in the field of financial control, it should be able in the medium term to use the Union's regional and structural funds for its development effectively.

For *agriculture*, particular efforts will be needed to implement veterinary and phytosanitary requirements and to strengthen the administrative structures necessary to apply the common agricultural policy instruments. Provided these targets can be met, accession in the medium term should not be accompanied by significant problems in applying the common agricultural policy in an appropriate manner.

On *energy*, the Czech Republic has a substantial nuclear power programme, which is due to expand further. The modernisation programme needed to bring the nuclear plants at Dukovny and Temelin up to internationally accepted safety standards must be completed within 7-10 years. The Czech Republic should be able to comply with the rest of the *acquis* in the medium term, given further work on energy pricing, state intervention in the solid fuel sector and access to networks.

On the basis of the analysis of its capacity to apply the *acquis*, the Czech Republic could be in a position in the medium term to take and implement the measures necessary for removal of controls at its *borders* with Member States of the Union. If part of its current borders became part of the Union's external border, reinforcement of border controls would be needed.

The Czech Republic's participation in the third stage of *Economic and Monetary Union*, which implies coordination of economic policy and complete liberalisation of capital movements, should pose no problems in the medium term. But it is premature to judge whether the Czech Republic will be in a position, by the time of its accession, to participate in the euro area. That will depend on how far the success of its structural transformation enables it to achieve and sustain permanently the convergence criteria. These are, however, not a condition for membership.

The Czech Republic is likely to comply with the *justice* and *home affairs acquis* in the next few years, provided that existing progress is maintained, including in the fight against drugs and organised crime.

The Czech Republic should be able to fulfil its obligations in respect of the *common foreign* and *security policy*.

In addition, the Czech Republic has no territorial disputes with any member state or neighbouring candidate country. All its state frontiers are regulated by Treaty. There remain some minor issues in its relationship with Slovakia.

4) Administrative and Legal Capacity

For the Czech Republic to have in the medium term the administrative structures necessary for the essential work of applying and enforcing the *acquis* effectively, there will need to be a significant and sustained effort of reform.

It is not yet possible to judge when the Czech Republic's judicial system, which has an equally important role to play, will acquire the capacity to play it effectively, though reform will clearly be required.

Conclusion

In the light of these considerations, the Commission concludes that:

☐ the Czech Republic presents the characteristics of a democracy, with stable institutions guaranteeing the rule of law, human rights and respect for and protection of minorities;

☐ the Czech Republic can be regarded as a functioning market economy, and it should be able to cope with competitive pressure and market forces within the Union in the medium term;

☐ if the Czech Republic continues its efforts on transposition of the *acquis* relating to the Single Market and intensifies work on its implementation, the Czech Republic should become capable in the medium term of applying it fully. The import deposit scheme will need to be resolved within the terms of the Europe Agreement. Particular effort, including investment, will be needed to meet the *acquis* in sectors such as agriculture, environment and energy. Further administrative reform will be indispensable if the Czech republic is to have the structures to apply and enforce the *acquis* fully.

In the light of these considerations, the Commission recommends that negotiations for accession should be opened with Czech Republic.

The reinforced pre-accession strategy will help the Czech Republic to prepare itself better to meet the obligations of membership, and to take action to improve the shortcomings identified in this Opinion. The Commission will present a report no later than the end of 1998 on the progress it has achieved.

Annex

Present Composition of the Parliament of the Czech Republic

Political Party		Chamber		Senate	
		Seats	%	Seats	%
Civil Democratic Party	ODS	68	33	32	39.5
Civic Democratic Alliance	ODA	13	7	7	8.6
Christian Democratic Party	KDU-CSL	18	9	13	16.0
Social Democratic Party	CSSD	61	31	25	30.8
Republican Party	SPR-RSC	18	11		
Communist Party of Bohemia and Moravia	KSCM	22	9	2	2.5
Democratic Union	DEU				1.2
Independents					1.2
		200		81	

Single Market: White Paper Measures

This table is based on information provided by the Czech authorities and confirmed by them as correct as at the end of June 1997. It does not indicate the Commission's agreement with their analysis. The table includes directives and regulations cited in the White Paper which total 899. These have been listed in accordance with the categorization used in the White Paper and in relation to the policy areas covered. The table shows the number of measures for which the Czech Republic authorities have notified the existence of adopted legislation having some degree of compatibility with the corresponding White Paper measures.

White Paper chapters		Directives Stage I	Directives Stage II/III	Regulations Stage I	Regulations Stage II/III	Total
1. Free movement of capital	Czech Republic	0	1	0	0	1
	Number of White Paper measures	3	1	0	0	4
2. FM and safety of industrial products	Czech Republic	34	24	2	0	60
	Number of White Paper measures	56	104	4	1	165
3. Competition	Czech Republic	3	0	0	0	3
	Number of White Paper measures	3	0	1	0	4
4. Social policy and action	Czech Republic	11	10	0	1	22
	Number of White Paper measures	12	15	0	2	29
5. Agriculture	Czech Republic	28	24	5	0	57
	Number of White Paper measures	93	46	62	2	203
6. Transport	Czech Republic	13	6	4	4	27
	Number of White Paper measures	19	15	8	13	55
7. Audio-visual	Czech Republic	1	0	0	0	1
	Number of White Paper measures	1	0	0	0	1
8. Environment	Czech Republic	5	5	2	1	13
	Number of White Paper measures	31	7	7	0	45
9. Telecommunication	Czech Republic	3	0	0	0	3
	Number of White Paper measures	9	7	0	0	16
10. Direct taxation	Czech Republic	1	1	0	0	2
	Number of White Paper measures	2	2	0	0	4
11. Free movement of goods	Czech Republic	0	0	0	0	0
	Number of White Paper measures	0	0	0	0	0
12. Public procurement	Czech Republic	0	5	0	0	5
	Number of White Paper measures	5	1	0	0	6
13. Financial services	Czech Republic	8	3	0	0	11
	Number of White Paper measures	13	8	0	0	21
14. Protection of personal data	Czech Republic	0	1	0	0	1
	Number of White Paper measures	0	2	0	0	2
15. Company law	Czech Republic	2	2	0	0	4
	Number of White Paper measures	2	3	0	1	6
16. Accountancy	Czech Republic	2	1	0	0	3
	Number of White Paper measures	3	2	0	0	5
17. Civil law	Czech Republic	1	0	0	0	1
	Number of White Paper measures	1	1	0	0	2
18. Mutual rec. of prof. qual	Czech Republic	2	0	0	0	2
	Number of White Paper measures	2	16	0	0	18
19. Intellectual property	Czech Republic	5	2	0	0	7
	Number of White Paper measures	5	3	0	0	11
20. Energy	Czech Republic	1	1	0	0	2
	Number of White Paper measures	10	2	3	0	15
21. Customs law	Czech Republic	1	1	23	157	182
	Number of White Paper measures	2	1	14	184	201
22. Indirect taxation	Czech Republic	0	4	0	0	4
	Number of White Paper measures	15	54	0	6	75
23. Consumer protection	Czech Republic	5	1	0	0	6
	Number of White Paper measures	8	3	0	0	11
Total	Czech Republic	126	92	36	163	417
	Number of White Paper measures	295	293	99	212	899

Statistical Data

If not explicitly stated otherwise, data contained in this annex are collected from *Czech Statistical Office* (Cesky Statisticky Úrad) with whom Eurostat and Member States' statistical offices are co-operating since several years in the framework of the PHARE programme. Regular data collection and dissemination are part of this co-operation process with the aim to enable the application of EU laws and practices in statistics. The data presented below have been compiled as far as possible using EU definitions and standards which in some cases differ from national practices. This may occasionally give rise to differences between the data presented here and those shown elsewhere in the opinion, which are generally based on the individual applicant countries' updated replies to the questionnaire sent to them in April 1996. The exact compatibility with EU standards on statistics and thus the comparability with EU figures can still not be guaranteed, particularly those statistics that have not been supplied through Eurostat, but have been delivered directly by the countries concerned. The exact compatibility with EU standards on statistics and thus the comparability with EU figures can still not be guaranteed. Wherever available, methodological notes are given describing content and particularities of statistical data presented in this annex. Data correspond to the information available as of May 1997.

Basic Data

	1990	1992	1993	1994	1995
	\multicolumn{5}{c}{In 1 000 hectares}				
Total area			7 886	7 887	7 887
Population (end of the period)	\multicolumn{5}{c}{In 1 000}				
Total		10 326	10 334	10 333	10 321
Females			5 311.7	5 311.2	5 305
Males			5 022.3	5 021.8	5 016
	\multicolumn{5}{c}{Per 1 km²}				
Population density			131	131	131	131
	\multicolumn{5}{c}{In % of total population}				
Urban population			69.6	67.5	74.7	74.7
	\multicolumn{5}{c}{Per 1 000 of population}				
Deaths rate			11.7	11.5	11.4	11.4
Births rate			11.8	11.7	10.3	9.3
Income and GDP per capita	\multicolumn{5}{c}{In European Currency Unit}				
Average monthly wage and salary per employee					235
GDP per capita					3 491
Structure of production: share of branch GVA	\multicolumn{5}{c}{In % of total Gross Value Added}				
Agriculture	7.5				5.2
Industry	50.0				34.1
Construction	8.3				7.3
Services	34.2				53.4

Share of branch GVA in 1990

- Agriculture: 7.5%
- Industry: 50.0%
- Construction: 8.3%
- Services: 34.2%
- Others: 0.0%

Share of branch GVA in 1995

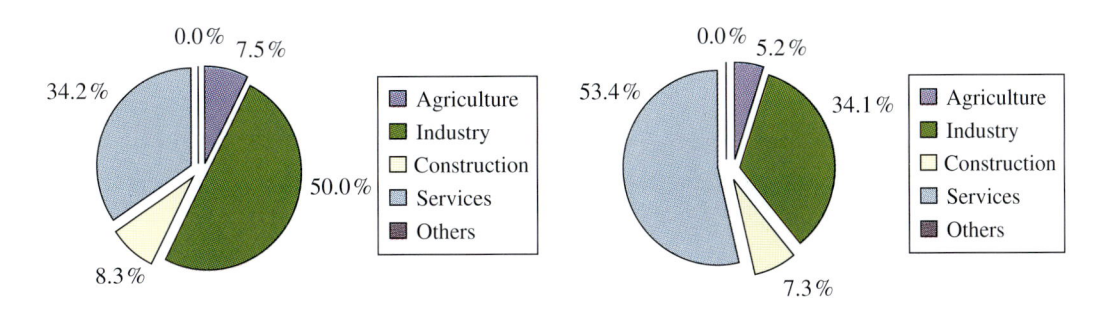

- Agriculture: 5.2%
- Industry: 34.1%
- Construction: 7.3%
- Services: 53.4%
- Others: 0.0%

National Accounts

	1990	1991	1992	1993	1994	1995
	\multicolumn{6}{c}{In millions of national currency}
Gross Domestic Product (current prices)	567 300	716 600	791 000	1 096 807	1 139 221	1 252 100
	\multicolumn{6}{c}{In billions of ECU}
Gross Domestic Product (current prices)				32.1	33.3	36.1
	\multicolumn{6}{c}{In purchasing power standard per capita}
Gross Domestic Product				8 749.0	9 698.0	9 410.0
	\multicolumn{6}{c}{% Change over the previous year}
Gross Domestic Product	− 1.2	− 14.2	− 6.4	− 0.9	2.6	4.8
Final consumption expenditure	4.9	− 22.8	8.9	2.0	3.0	3.4
Of households and NPISH	6.7	− 28.5	15.1	2.9	5.4	6.1
Of general government	0.9	− 9.0	− 3.1	− 0.1	− 2.6	− 3.7
Gross fixes capital formation	− 2.1	− 17.7	8.9	− 7.7	17.3	16.1
Exports of goods and services			6.8	7.5	0.2	7.9
Imports of goods and services			22.0	10.4	7.8	19.2
	\multicolumn{6}{c}{In % of Gross Domestic Product}
Final consumption expenditure	69.9	63.3	71.3	69.8	67.6	76.7
Of households and NPISH	50.6	44.8	50.9	48.1	46.4	57.3
Of general government	19.4	18.5	20.4	21.7	21.2	19.4
Gross fixed capital formation	28.6	29.9	28.2	27.5	27.5	31.0
Exports of goods and services		57.5	53.4	51.5	51.4	59.3
Imports of goods and services		50.7	54.1	50.2	52.8	63.8

GDP (% Change over the previous year)

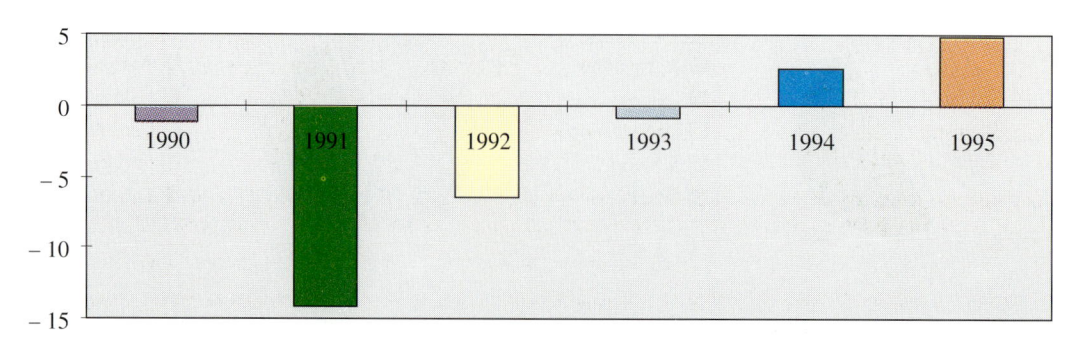

Final consumption expenditure: final consumption expenditure of households and Non Profit Institution Saving Households (NPISH) in 1990/1991 exclude NPISH. Final consumption expenditure of general government in 1990/1991 include NPISH.

Main Economic Indicators

	1990	1991	1992	1993	1994	1995	1996
	\multicolumn{7}{c	}{In percentage change over the previous year}
Inflation rate	9.7	56.5	11.1	20.8	10	9.1	8.8
	\multicolumn{7}{c	}{Previous year = 100}
Industrial production volume indices				94.7	102.1	109.2	106.8
Gross agricultural production volume indices				97.7	94.0	105.0	
Unemployment rate (ILO methodology)	\multicolumn{7}{c	}{In % labour force}
Total				3.9	3.8	3.6	3.4
Less then 25 years					7.7	6.8	6.1
25 years and more					3	2.9	2.9
	\multicolumn{7}{c	}{In billions of USD}
Gross foreign debt				4 548	5 838		
Balance of payments	\multicolumn{7}{c	}{In millions of USD}
Exports of goods				12 997.2	14 016.4	21 462.4	21 702.5
Imports of goods				– 13 308.9	– 14 905.3	– 25 140.3	– 27 674.3
Trade balance				– 311.8	– 888.8	– 3 677.8	– 5 971.8
Services, net				1 010.7	733.0	1 842.0	1 785.1
Income, net				– 117.4	– 20.2	– 105.7	– 679.9
Current account balance				669.2	– 49.7	– 1 369.1	– 4 476.4
Capital and fin. acc. (excl. reserves)				2 470.0	3 371.1	8 232.6	4 072.3
Reserve assets				– 3 029.3	– 2 371.6	– 7 458.1	828.0

Inflation rate: percentage change of yearly average over the previous year — all items index (data are based on national CPIs which are not strictly comparable).

Industrial production volume indices: industrial production covers mining and quarrying, manufacturing and electricity, gas and water supply (according to the NACE Classification Sections C, D, E). In 1993/1994 the index of total industrial production is based on exhaustive surveying in enterprises with 25 or more employees, since 1995 with 100 or more employees; and on estimates proceeding from quarterly sample surveys for enterprises up to 24 (or 99) employees and for natural persons — tradesmen not registered in the Business Register. Indices for branches, however, cover only enterprises with 25 or more employees up to the end of 1994 and since 1995 with 100 or more.

Gross agricultural production volume indices: indices based on evaluation of all individual products of gross agricultural production. Constant prices refer to 1989.

Unemployment rate (by ILO methodology): percentage of the unemployed labour force. This rate is derived from LFSS (Labour Force Sample Survey) observing the following ILO definitions and recommendations.

Labour force: employed and unemployed persons in the sense of the ILO definitions stated below.

The employed: all persons aged 15+, who during the reference period worked at least one hour for wage or salary or other remuneration as employees, entrepreneurs, members of cooperatives or contributing family workers. Members of armed forces and women on child-care leave are included.

The unemployed: all persons aged 15+, who concurrently meet all three conditions of the ILO definition for being classified as the unemployed: a) have no work, b) are actively seeking a job and c) are ready to take up a job within a fortnight.

The persons on compulsory military service are excluded from the employed but women on additional child-care leave are included.

Gross foreign debt: debt is extracted form the OECD's External Debt Statistics.

Balance of payments: data is derived from IMF database, their comparability with respective EU statistics can not be guaranteed, but balance of payments is compiled mainly in accordance to IMF standards. Balance in trade of goods in accordance with balance of payments principles. Exports and imports are both in fob values. Net income includes direct, portfolio and other investment income, compensation of employees. Current account balance by definition of *IMF 5th Manual*, capital transfers are excluded. Reserve assets: it means changes in reserve assets during the year; (+) signifies an increase, (–) a decrease in reserve assets.

Foreign Trade

	1992	1993	1994	1995	1996
Imports and exports (current prices)		In millions of USD			
Imports		12 860	14 971	25 265	27 824
Exports		13 206	14 255	21 657	21 918
Balance of trade		346	− 716	− 3 608	− 5 906
External trade volume indices		Previous year = 100			
Imports		106.7	114.2	123.7	109.6
Exports		119.1	102.6	105.7	100.0
Structure of import trade by SITC (current prices)		In % of total import			
(0 + 1): food and live animals, beverage and tobacco	7.5	7.3	8.2	6.3	6.5
2: crude materials, inedible	5.8	5.0	4.9	4.5	3.7
3: mineral fuels and lubricants	15.5	11.1	10.0	7.8	8.7
4: animal and vegetable oils etc.	0.3	0.4	0.4	0.3	0.3
5: chemicals and related products	9.8	12.1	13.1	11.8	11.8
6: manufactured goods classified chiefly by material	10.3	15.9	16.5	20.3	19.3
7: machinery and transport equipment	41.5	36.1	35.0	37.1	38.2
8: miscellaneous manufactured articles	9.3	11.7	11.9	11.9	11.5
9: goods not elsewhere classified	0.0	0.4			
Structure of export trade by SITC (current prices)		In % of total export			
(0 + 1): food and live animals, beverage and tobacco	8.8	7.8	6.5	5.6	5.1
2: crude materials, inedible	6.5	6.1	6.8	5.2	4.7
3: mineral fuels and lubricants	5.7	6.2	5.7	4.3	4.5
4: animal and vegetable oils etc.	0.1	0.2	0.3	0.2	0.2
5: chemicals and related products	9.2	9.5	10.0	9.3	9.1
6: manufactured goods classified chiefly by material	32.3	29.9	30.5	32.2	28.8
7: machinery and transport equipment	25.4	27.6	25.9	30.4	32.7
8: miscellaneous manufactured articles	12.0	12.7	14.3	12.8	14.9
9: goods not elsewhere classified					
External trade price indices		Previous year = 100			
Imports		98.8	100.6	104.0	102.8
Exports		102.3	103.9	104.6	103.5

Imports and exports (current prices), external trade volume indices and structure of external trade by SITC (current prices): trade data exclude direct re-exports, trade in services and trade with customs free zones as well as licenses, know-how and patents. The data are based upon the special trade system and are regularly updated. For 1994: data uses the methodology in use up to the end of 1995. From year 1995 on: data uses the methodology in use just since January 1, 1996. *Trade Classifications:* the Czech Republic is using the commodity classification according to the Combined Nomenclature. *Imports* are recorded on *FOB* basis and are captured with the date the commodities are released into circulation in the country. *Exports* are recorded on *FOB* basis and are captured with the date on which the commodities cross the customs border. The customs statistics is utilized for monitoring of foreign trade data. Eurostat has converted National Currencies to the US dollar by applying the International Monetary Fund annual average exchange rates.

External trade price indices: the price indices have been calculated by 'unit value' method.

Foreign Trade

	1992		1993		1994		1995		1996	
Structure of imports by main countries (current prices)	In % of total imports									
1st partner	D	26.3	D	25.4	D	25.5	D	25.8	D	29.8
2nd partner	RU	20.2	SK	17.4	SK	14.2	SK	13.1	SK	9.6
3rd partner	AT	9.1	RU	9.8	RU	8.4	RU	8.9	RU	7.4
4th partner	US	5.4	AT	7.8	AT	8.1	AT	6.9	I	5.9
5th partner	I/F	4.7	I	4.7	I	5.1	I	5.8	AT	5.7
Others		29.6		34.9		38.7		39.5		41.6
Structure of exports by main countries (current prices)	In % of total exports									
1st partner	D	33.3	D	26.0	D	29.4	D	31.8	D	35.9
2nd partner	RU	8.5	SK	21.5	SK	16.4	SK	16.2	SK	14.3
3rd partner	AT	7.4	AT	6.0	AT	7.1	AT	6.5	AT	6.5
4th partner	I	5.7	I	5.0	I	4.4	PL	5.4	PL	5.6
5th partner	PL	5.0	RU	4.5	RU	3.9	I	4.0	I	3.3
Others		40.1		37.0		38.8		36.1		34.4

Structure of export by main partners in 1996

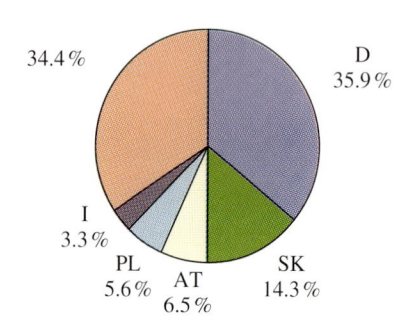

- D 35.9%
- SK 14.3%
- AT 6.5%
- PL 5.6%
- I 3.3%
- 34.4%

Structure of import by main partners in 1996

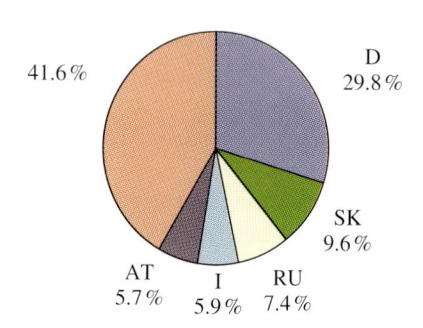

- D 29.8%
- SK 9.6%
- RU 7.4%
- I 5.9%
- AT 5.7%
- 41.6%

AT	Austria	PL	Poland
D	Germany	RU	Russian Federation
F	France	SK	Slovakia
I	Italy	US	United States

Social indicators

	1991	1992	1993	1994	1995
Population on 1 January	\multicolumn{5}{c}{In thousands}				
	10 304.61	10 312.55	10 325.7	10 334	10 333
Proportion of population by age 1 January 1995	\multicolumn{5}{c}{In % of total population}				
0 - 14 years					18.9
15 - 24 years					16.5
25 - 44 years					27.9
45 - 64 years					23.6
65 years and more					13.1
	\multicolumn{5}{c}{Total number}				
Live births	129 354	121 705	121 025	106 618	
Deaths	124 290	120 337	118 185	117 497	
Infant deaths					
Less than 1 year	1 343	1 204	1 020	847	
Still birth	496	437	445	336	
Marriages	71 973	74 060	66 033	58 440	
Divorces	29 366	28 572	30 227	30 939	
	\multicolumn{5}{c}{Per 1 000 of population}				
Crude marriage rate	7.00	7.20	6.40	5.70	5.3
Crude divorce rate	2.90	2.80	2.90	3.00	3.0
Natural growth	0.50	0.10	0.30	– 1.10	
Net migration	0.30	1.20	0.50	1.00	
Tota population growth	0.80	1.30	0.80	– 0.10	
Total fertility rate	1.86	1.70	1.70	1.40	
Infant mortality rate	10.38	9.89	8.40	7.90	7.7
Late foetal mortality rate	3.82	3.58	3.66	3.14	
Life expectancy	\multicolumn{5}{c}{At birth}				
Males		68.7	69.3	69.5	70.0
Females		76.6	76.4	76.6	76.9
Life expectancy	\multicolumn{5}{c}{At 65 years}				
Males					12.7
Females					16.2

Infant deaths: data for the year 1994: children born in 1993 and 1994 deceased before the age of 1 year in 1994.

Infant mortality rate: data for the year 1994: children born in 1993 and 1994 deceased before the age of 1 year in 1994.

Labour Market

	1993	1994	1995	1996
	\multicolumn{4}{c}{In percent of population age +15}			
Economic activity rate (ILO methodology)	63.3	63.3	62.8	62.6
	\multicolumn{4}{c}{In thousands}			
Average employment	3 420	3 369	3 123	3 030
Unemployment rate by age (ILO methodology)	\multicolumn{4}{c}{In % of labour force}			
Total	3.9	3.8	3.6	3.4
Less than 25 years		7.7	6.8	6.1
25 years and more		3.0	2.9	2.9
Registered unemployment (end of period)	\multicolumn{4}{c}{In % of economically active population}			
	3.5	3.2	2.9	3.5
Average paid employment indices by NACE classes	\multicolumn{4}{c}{Previous year = 100}			
Agriculture, hunting, forestry and fishing	82.5	87.4	80.2	95.3
Mining and quarrying	91.1	90.1	89.5	92.3
Manufacturing		95.3	88.7	96.4
Production and distribution of electricity, gas and water		102.7	97.5	98.2
Construction		104.5	100.2	98.7
Transport, storage and communication		96.6	98.7	98.9
Monthly nominal wages and salaries indices by NACE classes				
Agriculture, hunting, forestry and fishing	119.6	115.0	117.3	113.9
Mining and quarrying	117.0	113.2	114.8	115.8
Manufacturing	123.8	117.3	118.4	117.5
Production and distribution of electricity, gas and water	121.5	117.3	118.8	119.1
Construction	130.0	116.7	115.9	114.0
Transport, storage and communication	123.3	120.0	121.1	118.8
Monthly wages and salaries indices				
Nominal	125.3	118.5	118.5	118.0
Real	103.7	107.7	108.6	108.5

Economic activity rate (ILO Methodology): percentage of labor force in the total population aged 15+. This rate is derivated of LFSS (Labour Force Sample Survey) observing the following ILO definitions and recommendations.

Labour force: employed and unemployed persons in the sense of the ILO definitions stated below.

The employed: all persons aged 15+, who during the reference period worked at least one hour for wage or salary or other remuneration as employees, entrepreneurs, members of cooperatives or contributing family workers. Members of armed forces and women on child-care leave are included.

The unemployed: all persons aged 15+, who concurrently meet all three conditions of the ILO definition for being classified as the unemployed: a) have no work, b) are actively seeking a job and c) are ready to take up a job within a fortnight.

Unemployment rate (by ILO methodology): percentage of the unemployed labour force. This rate is derived from LFSS (Labour Force Sample Survey) observing the following ILO definitions and recommendations (See ILO definitions above).

The persons on compulsory military service are excluded from the employed but women on additional child-care leave are included.

Average employment and average paid employment indices by NACE classes: the data for entrepreneurial sphere cover organizations with 25 or more employees, since 1st quarter 1995 in industry, trade, catering and accommodation with 100 or more employees. The data cover also all budgetary, subsidised organisations and persons with secondary job are included. Armed forces, apprentices, employees on child-care and additional child-care leaves are excluded.

Registered unemployment (end of period): registered unemployment in per cent — percentage of unemployed registered in civil economically active population, based on Labour force sample survey (LFSS). Up to the 1st quarter 1994 economically active population based on administrative records (excl. armed forces); since the 2nd quarter 1994 economically active population includes persons in employment (incl. armed forces) based on LFSS, and registered unemployed persons.

Monthly wages and salaries indices: monthly *real* wages and salaries indices are derived from *gross* nominal wages and salaries indices divided by consumer price indices. The data for entrepreneurial sphere cover organizations with 25 or more employees, since 1st quarter 1995 in industry, trade, catering and accommodation with 100 or more employees. The data cover also all budgetary, subsidised organisations and persons with secondary job are included. Armed forces, apprentices, employees on child-care and additional child-care leaves are excluded.

Public Finance

	1990	1991	1992	1993	1994	1995
Government budget	\multicolumn{6}{c}{In billions of national currency}					
Government revenue				385.03	425.63	486.50
Grants						
Consolidated central government expenditure				383.32	441.21	499.36
Consolidated central government expenditure				445.12	521.27	596.35
Consolidated central government deficit/surplus				1.71	– 15.58	– 12.86
General government deficit/surplus				3.97	– 14.38	– 15.77
Government budget	\multicolumn{6}{c}{In % of Gross Domestic Product}					
Consolidated central government expenditure				42.1	42.5	41.2
Consolidated central government expenditure				48.9	50.2	49.2
Consolidated central government deficit/surplus				0.2	– 1.5	– 1.1
General government deficit/surplus				0.4	– 1.4	– 1.3

Government budget: these data relate to central and general government as published in the IMF's *Government Finance Statistics Yearbook (1996) (GFSY)*; included also is the country's presentation in the *GFSY*.

Because the *GFSY* does not present statistics for general government, but for individual levels of government separately, the consolidated series presented here were obtained from central and local government data and adjusted in consolidation for the identified intergovernmental transfers.

Even though the statistics cover the central and local government published in *GFSY*, the coverage may not be exhaustive if some central or local government units are not included in that coverage. A measure of the exhaustiveness of the coverage can be obtained by comparing in the *GFSY* the note on the coverage of data for individual countries with the list of central and local government units provided.

It should be noted that the deficit/surplus used here is equal to revenue and grants minus expenditure, and does not take lending minus repayments into account (see further below).

The netting of inter-government transfers carried-out in the attached tables is limited to the current and capital transfers consisting of the identified grants and current and capital subsidies between the levels of government. Other types of transactions occurring between government levels, such as the payments of taxes and employers' social security contributions, and the reciprocal purchases of goods and services are not normally classified as inter-governmental transfers have not been eliminated in the consolidation process. Finally, whether the absence of data for current and capital transfers should be attributed to the absence of transfer or to lack of data is unclear; in all cases absence of information on transfers have been deemed to represent zero-transfers.

a) *Government expenditure* consists of general government cash expenditures on current and capital goods and services, interest payments and current and capital transfers but excludes non-cash transactions.

b) *Deficit/surplus* equals cash revenue and cash grants minus cash expenditure. This measure of the deficit/surplus differs from that used in *GFS* which equals cash revenue and cash grants, minus cash expenditure, minus net lending. This exclusion of net lending (consisting, in the *GFS* methodology, of operations in financial assets and liabilities carried out for specific policy purposes, rather than for liquidity purposes) brings the measure of the deficit/surplus presented here closer to the national accounts concept of net borrowing/net lending. Also, as a result of this exclusion, receipts from privatisation (classified as repayments in the *GFS* methodology) do not enter in the determination of the deficit/surplus presented in the attached tables (and therefore do not reduce the deficit).

Financial Sector

	1990	1991	1992	1993	1994	1995	1996
Monetary aggregates	\multicolumn{7}{c}{In billions (10^9) of US dollars}							
Monetary aggregate M1				12.01	15.04	17.04	17.39
Quas-money				12.03	15.99	22.04	23.61
	\multicolumn{7}{c}{In millions (10^6) of US dollars}						
Total reserves (gold excluded, end of period)				3 789	6 145	13 843	12 297
Average short term interest rates	\multicolumn{7}{c}{In % per annum}						
Lending rate				14.07	13.12	12.80	12.54
Deposit rate				7.03	7.07	6.96	6.79
Official discount rate (end of period)					8.50	9.50	10.50
USD exchange rates	\multicolumn{7}{c}{1 USD = ... CZK}						
Average of period				29.153	28.785	26.541	27.145
End of period				29.955	28.049	26.602	27.332
ECU exchange rates	\multicolumn{7}{c}{1 ECU = ... CZK}						
Average of period				34.138	34.240	34.716	34.715
End of period				33.420	34.501	34.961	34.247

Monetary aggregates: *money (M1):* includes demand deposits and currency outside banks. *Quasi money (QM):* includes time, savings and foreign currency deposits. Eurostat has converted National Currencies to the US dollar by applying the International Monetary Fund annual end of period exchange rates.

Total reserves (gold excluded, end of period): the statistics on official foreign reserves are extracted from the IMF's monthly *International Financial Statistics (IFS)*. Total reserves (gold excluded) are defined as the sum of central bank holdings of foreign currencies and other (gross) claims on non-residents; this definition excludes claims on residents denominated in foreign currency. According to the definition; official foreign reserves are calculated at market exchange rates and prices in force at the end of the period under consideration. Total reserves (gold excluded) published in IFS may differ from the figures published by the national authorities. Some factors contributing to possible differences are the valuation of the reserve position in the Fund, and a different treatment of claims in non-convertible currencies.

USD exchange rates: International Monetary Fund exchange rates as present in the publication: *Statistiques financières internationales*.

Average short term interest rates: data are extracted from the IMF's monthly *International Financial Statistics (IFS)*. Average short-term lending and deposit rates relate to period averages. *Lending rates* generally consist of the average interest rate charged on loans granted by reporting banks. *Deposit rates* relate to average demand and time deposit rates or average time deposit rates. These rates may not be strictly comparable across countries to the extent the representative value of the reporting banks and the weighting schemes vary.

Inflation (twelve months changes)

Percentage change of the CPIs with the current month compared with the corresponding month of the previous year (t/t − 12).

	Jan.	Feb.	March	April	May	June	July	Aug.	Sept.	Oct.	Nov.	Dec.
1993	21.2	21.9	21.8	22.0	21.7	21.8	21.2	21.5	20.9	20.0	18.0	18.3
1994	11.0	9.7	9.4	9.1	9.3	9.6	9.7	10.2	10.5	10.7	10.6	10.1
1995	8.9	9.4	9.5	10.1	10.2	10.0	9.6	8.9	8.6	8.1	8.1	7.8
1996	8.9	8.6	8.9	8.6	8.7	8.4	9.4	9.6	8.8	8.6	8.6	8.6

Inflation (% change of CPI)

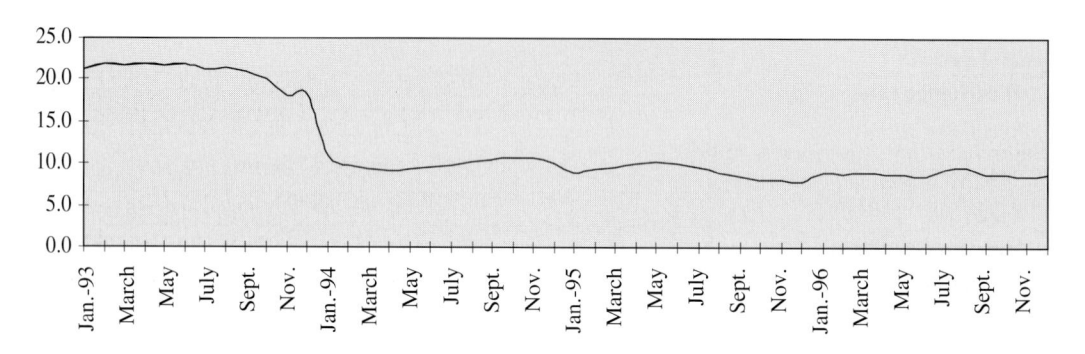

Inflation (twelve months changes): inflation rates (twelve months changes) are percentage changes of the CPIs with the current month compared with the corresponding month of the previous year. Inflation rates are based on national which are not strictly comparable between candidate countries or with those based on EU HICPs (different methods, concepts, practices in the calculation of CPIs).

Industry

	1993	1994	1995	1996
Structure of GDP by economic activities (NACE, current price)	\multicolumn{4}{c}{In % of Gross Domestic Product}			
Mining and quarrying	3.7	2.8	2.4	2.2
Manufacturing	26.7	26.3	26.6	26.6
Production and distribution of electricity, gas and water	6.6	5.7	5.1	5.0
Industrial production volume indices by NACE classes	\multicolumn{4}{c}{Previous year = 100}			
Total	94.7	102.1	109.2	106.8
Mining and quarrying	92.9	100.6	98.6	105.0
Manufacturing	92.3	100.1	108.2	105.5
Production and distribution of electricity, gas and water	95.2	97.2	103.4	102.5

	1993 Q1	1993 Q2	1993 Q3	1993 Q4	1994 Q1	1994 Q2	1994 Q3	1994 Q4
Industrial production volume indices by NACE classes	\multicolumn{8}{c}{Corresponding period of the previous year = 100}							
Total		96	93	95	99	101.6	106.2	102.6
Mining and quarrying		92	93	96	98	97.6	106.4	101.3
Manufacturing		94	90	91	98	100.6	102.9	99.3
Production and distribution of electricity, gas and water		95	97	99	88	96.3	94.8	110.6

1995 Q1	1995 Q2	1995 Q3	1995 Q4	1996 Q1	1996 Q2	1996 Q3	1996 Q4
\multicolumn{8}{c}{Corresponding period of the previous year = 100}							
108.2	107.4	107.6	113.2	109.7	106.6	109.1	102.6
97.1	95.6	100.5	101.0	110.1	102.4	114.0	95.5
106.4	105.8	106.7	113.7	107.4	105.0	108.9	101.3
102.9	104.3	101.8	104.3	109.8	97.9	105.9	96.9

Structure of GDP by economic activities (NACE, current prices): is calculated **at factor costs.**

Industrial production volume indices by NACE classes: industrial production covers mining and quarrying, manufacturing and electricity, gas and water supply (according to the NACE Classification Sections C, D, E). In 1993/1994 the index of total industrial production is based on exhaustive surveying in enterprises with 25 or more employees, since 1995 with 100 or more employees; and on estimates proceeding from quarterly sample surveys for enterprises up to 24 (or 99) employees and for natural persons – tradesmen not registered in the Business Register. Indices for branches, however, cover only enterprises with 25 or more employees up to the end of 1994 and since 1995 with 100 or more.

Infrastructure

	1991	1992	1993	1994	1995
	\multicolumn{5}{c}{In km per 1 000 km^2}
Railway network	119.9	119.7	119.8	119	120
Railway transport	\multicolumn{5}{c}{In million ton or passengers-km}
Freight transport			25 579	24 401	25 459
Passengers transport			8 548	8 481	8 023
	\multicolumn{5}{c}{In 1 000 of population}
Number of telephone subscribers	303	314	324	342	360
	\multicolumn{5}{c}{In inhabitants}
Number of inhabitants per passenger car	4.2	4.1	3.5	3.5	3.3

Agriculture

	1992	1993	1994	1995	1996
Land area by land-use categories	\multicolumn{5}{c}{In 1 000 hectares}				
Total	7 886	7 887	7 887	7 887	7 887
Agricultural land	4 283	4 282	4 281	4 280	
Forest	2 629	2 629	2 630	2 630	
Arable land	3 175	3 173	3 158	3 143	
Permanent meadows and pastures	872	873	886	902	
Agricultural land by legal status			In % of agricultural land		
State enterprise			14.0	4.5	
Cooperatives			49.6	41.9	
Others			36.4	53.6	
Share of GDP			In % of Gross Domestic Product		
Agriculture, hunting foresty and fishing (Nace A+B)		6.5	5.8	5.2	5
			Previous year = 100		
Gross agricultural production volume indices		97.7	94	105	99.8
Main crops by area			In 1 000 hectares		
Cereals	1 589	1 607	1 660	1 580	1 583.1
of which: wheat	759	783	812	832	799.0
Potatoes	111	105	77	78	85.0
Sugar beet	125	107	91	94	104.0
Fodder beet	10	12	12	12	
Main crops by yield			In 100 kg/hectares		
Cereals		41.3	40.3	40.8	41.8	42.0
of which: wheat		45.0	42.2	45.7	46.0	46.7
Potatoes		177.4	228.2	159.9	170.5	211.8
Sugar beet		309.7	402.6	356.0	394.9	415.0
Fodder beet		339.0	445.8	353.5	374.9	377.3
Sales or procurement of animal for slaughter			In 1 000 tons of live weight		
Pigs	536.1	582.2	515.0	565.8	607.0
Cattle	402.8	390.3	313.3	322.9	310.4
Poultry	153.2	113.3	109.9	140.0	132.1
Livestock breeding intensity (end of period)		In heads per 1 000 ha of agricultural land			
Cattle		523	474	465	445
of which: cows		200	179	178	168
Sheep		50	45	29	26
		In heads per 1 000 ha of arable land			
Pigs		1 287	1 220	1 210	1 290
of which: sows		93	92	97	

Share of GDP is calculated **at factor costs**.

Gross agricultural production volume indices: indices based on evaluation of all individual products of gross agricultural production. Constant prices refer to 1989.

Sales or procurement of animals for slaughter: the data refer to the **sales** of principal products of agriculture.

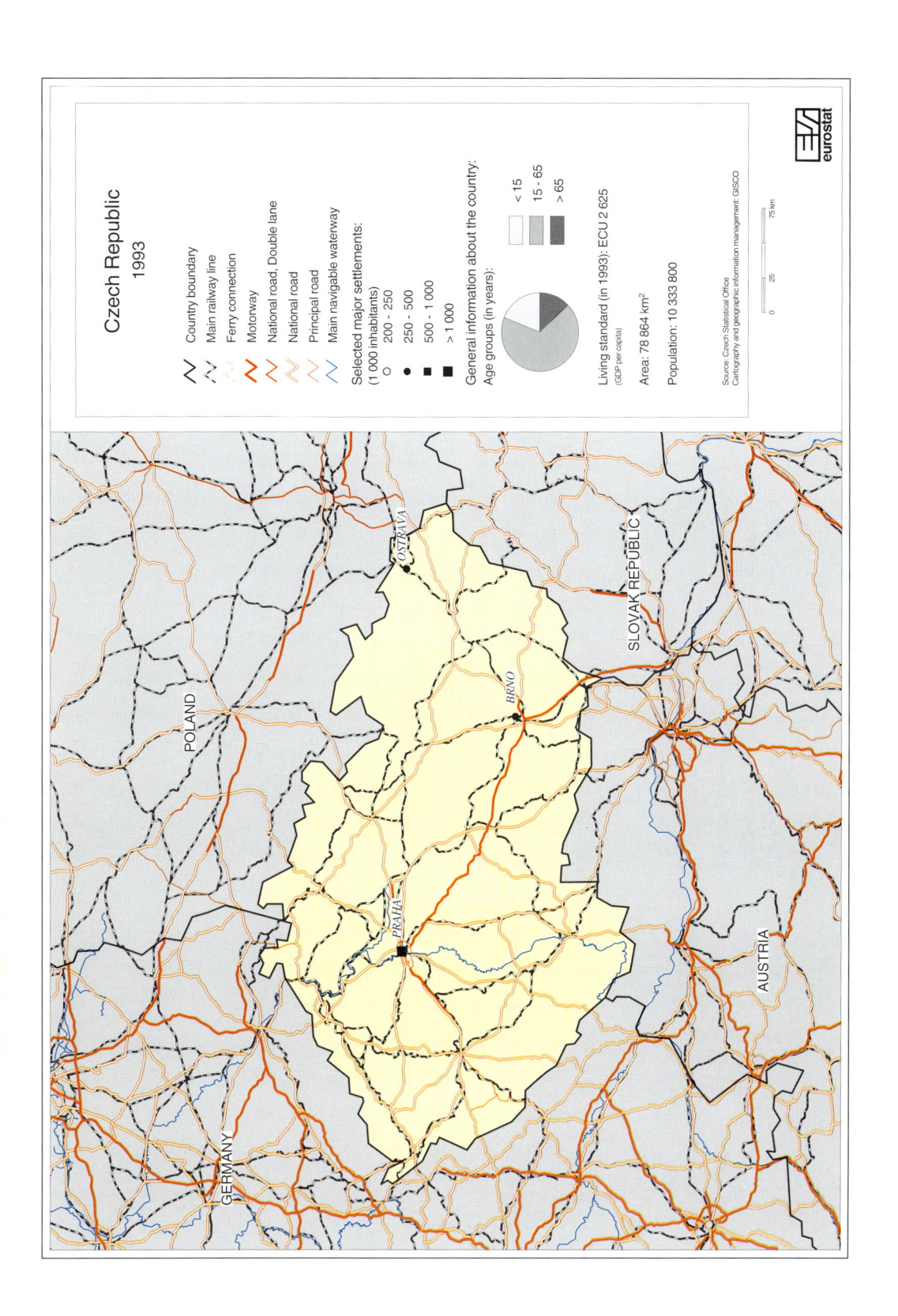

Czech Republic
1993

Country boundary
Main railway line
Ferry connection
Motorway
National road, Double lane
National road
Principal road
Main navigable waterway

Selected major settlements:
(1 000 inhabitants)
 200 - 250
 250 - 500
 500 - 1 000
 > 1 000

General information about the country:
Age groups (in years):
< 15
15 - 65
> 65

Living standard (in 1993): ECU 2 625
(GDP per capita)

Area: 78 864 km²

Population: 10 333 800

Source: Czech Statistical Office
Cartography and geographic information management: GISCO

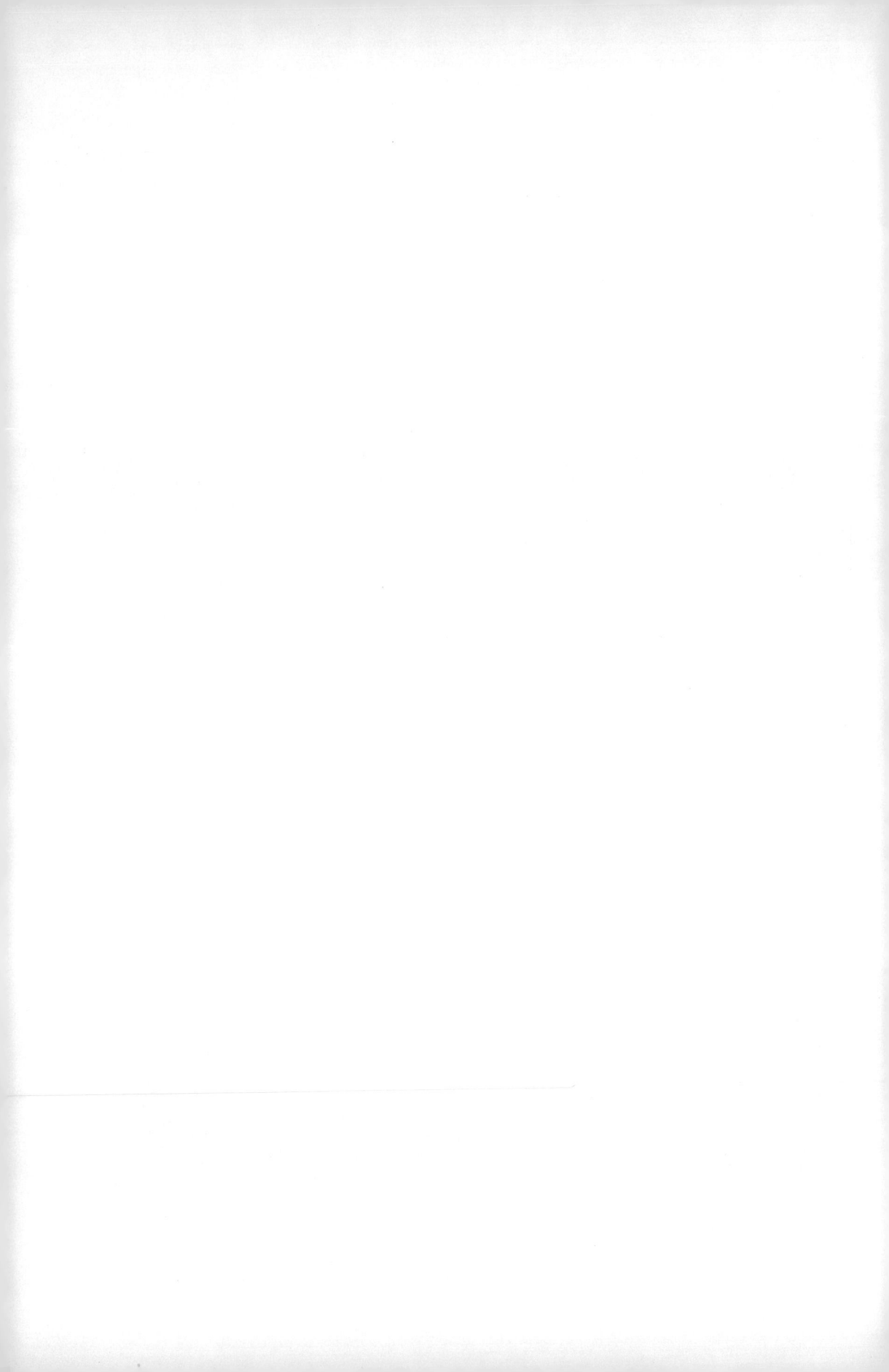

European Commission

Commission opinion on the Czech Republic's application for membership of the European Union

Supplement 14/97 to the Bulletin of the European Union

Luxembourg: Office for Official Publications of the European Communities

1997 — 107 pp. — 17.6 × 25.0 cm

ISBN 92-828-1226-X

Price (excluding VAT) in Luxembourg: ECU 7